DIGITAL: DISRUPT OR DIE

Mark J. Barrenechea
Tom Jenkins

Barrenechea, Mark J.
Jenkins, Tom

Digital: Disrupt or Die

First Printing, November 2014
Printed in Canada
First Edition

ISBN
978-0-9936047-3-7

$29.00 U.S.

Published by
Open Text Corporation
275 Frank Tompa Drive
Waterloo, Ontario, Canada
N2L 0A1
(519) 888-7111
info@opentext.com
www.opentext.com

ACKNOWLEDGEMENTS

*This book is dedicated to the staff, partners,
and customers of OpenText and
its subsidiaries. This book is possible due to their
combined efforts, innovation, and collective vision.*

We would like to thank the staff, users, and partners of
OpenText for their contributions to this book.

Special thanks go to writers Elizabeth Hanson and Sharon Malloch, editor Rebecca Graves,
and the following contributors:

Tania Almond, Eric Bencina, Travis Cain, Steven Cohen, Margaret Dobbin, Sonia Florez,
Sal Hakimi, Pat Harper, Kasey Holman, Steven Keifer, Ron Kelly, Barbara Kennedy,
Lisa Kyte, Ricky Lai, Lindsay Lane, Robin Lane, Nicole Lavell, Christine Lesden, Paul Loomis,
Dennis Lund, Deborah Miller, Mark Morley, Stefanie Nastou, Tom Niedoba, Melissa Noto,
Russ O'Neill, Donna Pearson, Lubor Ptacek, Beau Radloff, Ali Saleh, Anabel Sarrate,
Ray Schultz, Scott Schultz, Erin Schwab, Brandy Schwartz, Tim Spadzinski, Michele Stevenson,
Kathleen White, and Neil Wilson.

We would also like to thank Kevin Sy and Joe Dwyer for layout, design, and production.
Special thanks go out to all our customers as well for their contributions to this book.

Special resources are accredited in the Bibliography.

CONTENTS

FOREWORD

There's no denying the fact that the nature of business has changed significantly in the past decade. The rise of global markets, regulatory shifts, economic uncertainty, varying demographics, increasingly savvy consumers, and disruptive technologies has accelerated the pace of change into the 21st century.

In a digital-first world, many of the traditional channels and the organizations that control them have already become irrelevant. The Internet has almost obliterated barriers to entry, and cottage industries and niche markets are set to flourish. Globalization is introducing massive volumes of trade, an increasing number of regulations, and the opportunity for emerging economies like Brazil, Russia, India, and China (collectively known as BRIC) to evolve into dominant centers of economic influence. As trade increases, more and more physical products will be digitized into virtual goods. As a result, there will be higher rates of goods and activities that have a virtual component—involving Research and Development (R&D) skills and expertise and the exchange of information.

Enabled by technologies like mobile phones, social media, and the cloud, the exchange of digital information has grown significantly and the implications of this are profound. Technologies that have appeared on the horizon today will become prevalent and impose additional requirements for the enterprise to collect, govern, process, and protect its information for true competitive advantage.

Information is the new currency that fuels business growth. In 2020 business leaders will be required to develop and execute on strategies for information management, including robust capabilities for governance and compliance, to help the enterprise maximize the value of its information, while minimizing risk. For many organizations, finding this balance will be critical for survival. Between now and 2020, successful businesses will be those that adopt Enterprise Information Management (EIM) technologies and processes to ensure that their information assets are well-managed and secure.

To thrive in a rapidly evolving business environment, businesses across all industries must take steps beyond increasing efficiencies, reducing costs, improving governance, and strengthening management. To remain profitable, organizations should be prepared to exit their key businesses, embrace new consumer markets, introduce new products and services, and invest in human capital to manage business models that are in flux. The effective management of information makes this transformation possible.

This book has been written to give organizations an in-depth understanding of the ways in which their strategies and operations are being disrupted, and to provide them with the steps they can take to capitalize on opportunities to create value.

The journey is already underway. The road to empowering the enterprise to compete and lead in a digital-first world is a long and complex one. The outcome is clear—to digitize and disrupt or die.

This is our vision for 2020.

John Doolittle
CHIEF FINANCIAL OFFICER,
OPENTEXT CORPORATION

INTRODUCTION

"Use of digital technology is going to explode. The way we do business, the way customers interact with us, the nature of consumption–everything is going to change, and that presents huge opportunity."[1]

Business in a Digital-First World

A digital-first world is fast approaching. In every sector, digital technologies are already changing the rules of business by enabling new business models and leveling the playing field. In the past, technology has been fundamental in helping organizations reduce costs and increase productivity. While this is still the case, digitization is dramatically changing our business landscape with the promise of increased opportunity and innovation. Technology is transforming the very nature of business today, making it more fluid, social, global, accelerated, risky, and competitive.

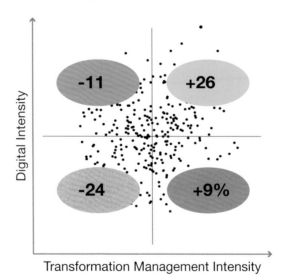

Digital Leaders are 26% More Profitable than Competitors[2]

[1] Accenture, *"CEO Briefing 2014"*, Global Agenda, 2014.

[2] Gapgemini Consulting and the MIT Center for Digital Business, *"The Digital Advantage: How digital leaders outperform their peers in every industry"*, 2012.

Most business leaders are well aware of the promise of rapid technological change. In 2020, CIOs, CMOs, CEOs, and line-of-business managers will be tasked with finding new customers, new markets, and new revenue streams using digital channels. The winners will successfully reinvent their businesses to thrive in a digital economy. Companies that demonstrate digital maturity will have higher financial performance than their less digitally mature competitors. On average, digital leaders are 26 percent more profitable than their industry competitors. They generate 9 percent more revenue through their employees and physical assets. And they create more value, generating 12 percent higher market valuation rates. For large, traditional companies, this can equate to billions of dollars.[3]

Disrupt or Die

All of the great innovators of today have embraced digital disruption. There are examples of it in every industry, as the winners overtake the established market leaders who fail to embrace new developments and opportunities fueled by disruptive digital technologies:

- In 2012, the **United States Postal Service (USPS)** was losing $25 million *every single day*[4], its service eclipsed by free Internet email like Google's Gmail® and fast, reliable delivery services from competitors like UPS®. People want direct and targeted services with immediate gratification, an outcome they receive when they send emails or pay their bills online. As we move toward becoming a paperless society, the USPS in its current incarnation (kept afloat by government funding) is bound to become obsolete.

- While Netflix®'s leadership anticipated the streaming trend in home video viewing, **Blockbuster**® was pursuing additional revenue streams by selling candy and popcorn in its stores.[5] As the largest American-based provider of home movie and video game rental services, at its peak Blockbuster boasted 60,000 employees and more than 9,000 stores. It failed to transform itself from its established bricks-and-mortar roots (declining the opportunity to purchase Netflix for $50 million in 2000) and was pushed out of its market by companies like Netflix and Redbox®. Blockbuster lost significant revenue and filed for bankruptcy on September 23, 2010. It closed its final stores in November of 2013.

---

[3] Gapgemini Consulting and the MIT Center for Digital Business, *"The Digital Advantage: How digital leaders outperform their peers in every industry"*, 2012.

[4] *"U.S. Postal Service in trouble, losing $25 million daily"* CNN, Dec 10, 2012, *http://outfront.blogs.cnn.com/2012/12/10/u-s-postal-service-in-trouble-losing-25-million-daily/* (accessed Jan 2014).

[5] Bernstein, Paula. *"Did Netflix Really Put Blockbuster Out of Business?"* Indiewire, February 4, 2014, *http://www.indiewire.com/article/did-netflix-put-blockbuster-out-of-business-this-infographic-tells-the-real-story* (accessed September 2014).

- Today, **Barnes & Noble**® is the last remaining national bookstore chain in the U.S. Its number one competitor is Amazon®. And while Amazon's stock price has risen by 50 percent since 1998, Barnes & Nobles' has fallen by 20 percent in the last decade.[6] Amazon sanctioned the market by digitizing its distribution: offering books for the same price but with better service that included convenient access to products, greater choice, peer reviews, recommendations, and sample downloads. Even before it moved into the market for e-books with the Kindle®, Amazon drove many booksellers out of business.

Apple Stock Price Vs HMV Stock Price[7]

- Iconic retailer and popular brand, **HMV** failed to explore new revenue streams or ways to offer convenient purchases and niche content, and finally delisted after its bankruptcy in January, 2013. Its major competitor, Apple's iTunes® is now a market dominator, offering entertainment as digital downloads to a massive audience. Bypassing its sales force, iTunes instantly connects millions of consumers to offer high accessibility and instant gratification. As one of the world's most valued brands, Apple's stock has risen by a staggering 6000 percent over the past 10 years.

[6] Accenture, "CEO Briefing 2014", Global Agenda, 2014
[7] Ibid.

- Canon® and Kodak® faced off in the digital arena, with Canon taking market share in 2005 through digital camera sales and **Kodak Eastman** losing $1.4 billion due to its slow transition to digital and a continued reliance on film for earnings. Kodak's portfolio ultimately failed in comparison to Canon's digital point-and-shoot camera, and after some costly restructuring, Kodak filed for bankruptcy in January 2012. It has recently emerged from bankruptcy (2013), reinventing itself as a commercial-printing company for business, leaving the consumer market altogether.[8] On an interesting note—as a representation of the profound shift that is taking place—while Kodak once employed 130,000 people to deliver its services; Instagram® does the same today with only 13 employees.

The business model that wins today is innovative, digital, and anticipates consumer need. Like Netflix, Amazon, and Apple, organizations that succeed will have to digitize the way they develop products and services, the way they market and sell, the way they distribute—the entire customer journey—or they'll be sidelined by their competition.

Key Disruptive Forces

Digital is coming. It's a very powerful, fast-moving train, fueled by key disruptors like cloud and mobile, a changing workforce, a digitized supply chain, digital consumers, and requirements to comply with increasing, global regulations.

In 2020, there will be larger, more interactive transactions and higher volume networking. New technologies like social and mobile, and how they are connected—over 5G networks—will change the way people experience the world. These networks will offer organizations zero-distance connectivity to a high-quality, global network of five billion users. Enterprise IT infrastructure will move to the cloud. Mobile users will replace PC users, and more services will be mobile-enabled. The Internet of Things (IoT) will automatically integrate machines, data, and people. Emerging technologies like three-dimensional (3-D) printing will radically change manufacturing by moving the entire supply chain online. By 2020, consumers will drive the majority of interactions with suppliers. Buyer-driven platforms will continue to infuse the digital-first world with dynamic and real-time results, expanding on Just-In-Time (JIT) manufacturing to optimize supply chains and meet customer demand.

---

[8] Beth Jinks, *"Kodak Moments Just a Memory as Company Exits Bankruptcy"*, Bloomberg.com, September 3, 2013, *http://www.bloomberg.com/news/2013-09-03/kodak-exits-bankruptcy-as-printer-without-photographs.html* (accessed July 2014).

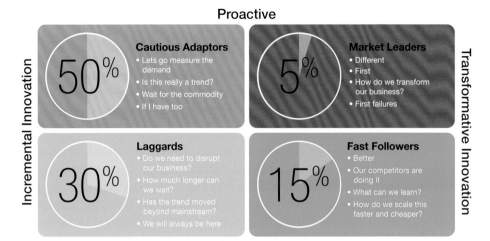

Proactive

Incremental Innovation | Transformative Innovation

Cautious Adaptors
50%
- Lets go measure the demand
- Is this really a trend?
- Wait for the commodity
- If I have too

Market Leaders
5%
- Different
- First
- How do we transform our business?
- First failures

Laggards
30%
- Do we need to disrupt our business?
- How much longer can we wait?
- Has the trend moved beyond mainstream?
- We will always be here

Fast Followers
15%
- Better
- Our competitors are doing it
- What can we learn?
- How do we scale this faster and cheaper?

Reactive

Market Leaders will Transform Their Businesses[9]

Internally, the enterprise of the future will have to support a culture of innovation and build technologies to support a changing workforce. At OpenText, we envisage that by the year 2020 our workforce will be dominated by digital natives—generations that have grown up with the Internet. We will have to cater to their needs. The concept of developing "on premise software", for example, will be archaic to future engineers. They will write a line of code for software that can be accessed and downloaded over the weekend. People won't wait a few years for software to be developed and implemented. Development cycles will happen in hyper-drive.

Finally, new technologies are requiring us to re-platform compliance. In 2020, growing regulatory and competitive pressures will require the enterprise to rethink and reprioritize its security and governance strategies for enterprise information. These requirements will be driven by emerging global regulations, increasing amounts of Internet users and privacy-related issues, big data, and protection against Intellectual Property (IP) loss.

[9] Wang, R., "The Building Blocks of Successful Corporate IT", Harvard Business Review, August 8, 2013, http://blogs.hbr.org/2013/08/the-building-blocks-of-success/ (accessed September 2014).

Now Is the Time to Capture Opportunity

Its hard to envision what technology will achieve. With its ability to transgress boundaries and overcome limitations, its possibilities are endless. Few people could have predicted the meteoric rise in popularity that the mobile device would have. Its applications are not fixed to its physical makeup as a phone: its uses are becoming more malleable. People are using their mobile phones in place of many other objects, from clocks, flashlights, maps, books, and cameras to entertainment centers, car keys, and personal assistants.

A digital-first world with new technologies, a changing workforce, a global marketplace, and digital consumers offers pure opportunity for the enterprise. The impact of its changes are just around the corner—only a handful of years away (which translates into just two years from an IT perspective). Now is the time to capture the opportunity and meet the challenges of a digital-first world. The pace of change in markets underlies the urgency with which the enterprise must transform itself into a digital enterprise.

Simplify, Transform, and Accelerate

But how can the enterprise effectively reinvent itself?

To succeed in 2020, the enterprise will have to simplify, transform, and accelerate its business. It can do so by reducing costs and increasing competitiveness through automated and digitized information processes. Consolidated information and process management empowers the digital enterprise to meet the requirements of a digital workforce and digital customers in a new disruptive world. To keep pace with accelerated innovation cycles, the enterprise must increase the speed of information delivery through integrated systems—on premise, in the cloud, and throughout its entire business network.

Information lies at the core of digital transformation. In a digital-first world, information is the new currency, playing a fundamental role in empowering the digital enterprise through innovation, growth, and opportunity. In 2020, organizations will be required to differentiate their products and services based on a strategy that maximizes the potential of information as a key differentiator.

This book has been written to help chart the course for the digital enterprise on its journey to a digital-first future. *Digital: Disrupt or Die* is a discourse on digital transformation. As told by our customers, analysts, innovators, and thought leaders, it describes a strategic multi-year blueprint for success in 2020.

Information leads to greater insights, better business decisions, higher customer satisfaction, greater agility, and optimized business performance. But how can the enterprise unlock the potential of information without compromising productivity and security?

Enterprise Information Management (EIM) is *the* key transformative technology. It provides a robust foundation for the digital enterprise to advance engagement with employees, customers, partners, and across the entire supply chain. This book explores the future of digital technologies, their impact on business, and how EIM equips the enterprise as it transforms itself to brace for change and opportunity in the year 2020 and beyond.

The way forward is clear. To successfully provide products and services to digital consumers, the enterprise must reinvent itself. With change comes tremendous opportunity: the opportunity for the enterprise to form deeper connections with its customers, partners, and employees; to create social, mobile and flexible workplaces that are conducive to higher levels of productivity and innovation; to deliver products and services according to individual need and specification; and to streamline the production and delivery of supply chains on a global scale. With opportunity comes risk, and the greatest risk is not embracing disruption in our increasingly digital society.

This book presents a systematic approach for the enterprise to re-conceptualize a digital-first future.

Are you ready?

Mark J. Barrenechea
PRESIDENT & CEO,
OPENTEXT CORPORATION

Tom Jenkins
CHAIRMAN,
OPENTEXT CORPORATION

DIGITAL DISRUPTION

CHAPTER 1
Digital Disruption

"The mindset of the digital disruptor accelerates every possible process by exploiting digital toolsets that are free for tinkering. Economists talk about trends that reduce barriers to entry. The force of digital disruption doesn't just reduce these barriers, it obliterates them."[1]

The pace of industry has accelerated. There have been more changes in the past twenty years than in the previous 100. In a world where everything is touched by technology, the enterprise has never had such an incredible opportunity to reinvent itself—to more closely align business with technology, deliver significant customer value, and make transformational business impact.

Changes that are taking place in business today are reminiscent of the seventies when technology promised increased competitive advantage through automation and greater efficiencies. Business models were radically transformed again in the nineties as technology and commerce intersected on the Internet. The technologies of today are causing seismic shifts in many industries, from publishing to entertainment to government. Old business models are being swept away as people find new ways to access information, news, entertainment, products, and services to meet their daily needs.

The year 2020 will see a convergence of technologies into a nexus that businesses can capitalize on to create true competitive edge. These forces run the gamut from cloud and social computing to mobile devices to the Internet of Things (IoT) and, when combined, they create a powerful platform for change. This chapter examines these digital technologies and how they will impact consumers, business, and society as a whole.

The Impact of Digital Technologies

Predicting the future is as fallible as forecasting the weather. To make predictions we look for cognitive clues, factor in experience, and defer to data. Despite the limited vision that characterizes human history, sometimes the forecasts are amazingly accurate. This is the case when we consider the theories of Clayton Christensen, Chris Anderson, and Gordon Moore.

---

[1] James McQuivey, *"Digital Disruption: Unleashing the Next Wave of Innovation"*, Forrester Research, Inc., 2013.

Spanning almost seven decades, these three men have helped to define the trajectory of digital innovation. Christensen coined the term "disruptive innovation". Moore (as in Moore's Law) described how technological innovations become affordable and mainstream. Anderson introduced the dynamic of the "long tail" to explain how niche markets thrive. According to all three, the future of digital innovation hinges on the Internet and disruptive technologies. When they are combined, these theories culminate in accelerated innovation and foretell an approaching digital industrial revolution.

Disruptive Innovation

Disruptive innovation is one of the most important theories to surface over the last twenty years. In his article for the Harvard Business Review (January - February 1995) *Disruptive Technologies: Catching the Wave*, Clayton Christensen defines the term *disruptive technology* (commonly referred to as *disruptive innovation*) as "an innovation that helps create a new market and value network, and eventually goes on to disrupt an existing market and value network (over a few years or decades), displacing an earlier technology."

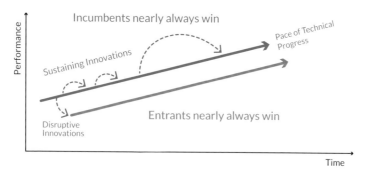

FIGURE 1.1: The Disruptive Innovation Model[2]

Disruptive innovation creates new markets or reshapes existing ones. As market leaders continue to produce sustaining technologies that are reliable and profitable, they create opportunities for disruptive innovations to enter the market. An innovation that is disruptive allows a niche set of customers to access a product or service that was at one time only accessible to consumers with a lot of money. Sound familiar? This premise lays the foundation for Chris Andersen's "Long Tail".

According to Christensen, disruptive technologies offer poorer performance than leading technologies but are more affordable and deliver benefits not currently available from existing technologies. Market leaders miss these innovations and how they will impact the market. In many instances, disruptive technologies quickly improve in quality and replace older technologies. In some cases, innovations enter the market and replace leading technologies immediately based on superior performance.

---

[2] Peter Duke, *"Sitting on Top of the World – A Strategy for Life (and Business)"*, Peter Duke Media Services, March 10, 2010, http://dukemedia.com/sitting-on-top-of-the-world/ (accessed Sept 2014).

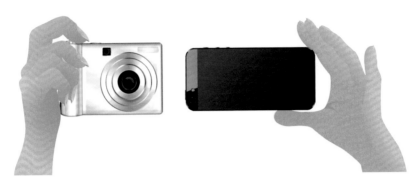

FIGURE 1.2: Digital Cameras Vs Mobile Phone Cameras

The mobile phone camera provides a great example of disruptive innovation. These cameras are becoming so advanced that they rival digital cameras. While smartphones have not yet surpassed standalone cameras in image quality, the gap between the two is lessening. As a result, digital camera companies have been forced to keep pace with mobile phone camera technology. The Nikon Cool Pix S800c®, for example, mimics a mobile phone by connecting to a Wi-Fi network so users can share their photos on social media sites. As this industry is reshaped by disruptive innovation, market leaders that fail to anticipate change risk becoming obsolete—a fate that Eastman Kodak suffered, filing for bankruptcy in 2012.

Moore's Law

Moore's Law is an attempt to describe the rapid pace of technological innovation. In 1965, Gordon Moore, the co-founder of Intel®, observed that the computer processors doubled in complexity every two years. He predicted that this trend would continue into the foreseeable future. Coined "Moore's Law", the theory posits that advances in technology are exponential, making devices more powerful every two years and half as expensive. As computers become more powerful, they become more accessible and can fuel further innovation. The Internet is the quintessential example of disruptive innovation. It has overhauled entire industries and continues to disrupt markets, both old and new.

The Long Tail

The Internet has democratized the means of production and distribution and facilitated Anderson's Long Tail. This theory is based on the economy moving away from producing mainstream products to satisfying niche markets. As the costs of production and distribution are driven down by the Internet, there is a declining demand for mass-produced goods. Customized niche markets can be successful and lucrative, based on a digitized supply chain. To break the theory down, the blue part of the graph below represents the mass production of goods that has dominated our culture for the last century. The orange part represents the long tail (or niche markets) and this is where the innovation is coming from now and into the future.

FIGURE 1.3: The Long Tail[3]

The swift pace of innovation gives digital disruptions even greater impact. For digital technology, this is based on the speed of development and the magnitude of innovation involved in its creation. Unlike the disruptions introduced by the web in the nineties, today's digital disruption is cheaper, faster, stronger, and reliant on the combination of key technologies and environmental factors. These include the ubiquity of mobile phones, increased speed and bandwidth, globalization, more affordable data storage, and faster computing power and data processing ability. With more people connected and sharing ideas in a global, digitized marketplace, the pace of innovation can only increase exponentially.

Digital Disruption is Stronger and Faster

FIGURE 1.4: Digital Disruption is Stronger and Faster[4]

---

[3] Chris Anderson, *"The Long Tail"*, *http://www.longtail.com/about.html* (Accessed May 2014).

[4] James McQuivey, *"Digital Disruption: Unleashing the Next Wave of Innovation"*, Forrester Research, 2013.

Based on this trajectory of innovation, in the year 2020 we will see the boundaries between technology and people blur, heightened by holographic TVs, three-dimensional (3-D) printing and manufacturing, and wearable technologies. Whole industries will be affected by the consolidation of information from diverse systems, including mobile devices, Global Positioning System (GPS), sensors, and video surveillance. All of these inputs will be connected and placed onto networks to contribute to the Internet of Things (IoT). Once they are integrated and accessible, these technologies will significantly transform market dynamics in all sectors.

2020: A Nexus of Forces

When combined, disruptive technologies like mobile computing, fifth-generation (5G) wireless networks, cloud computing, and the IoT form a "Nexus of Forces"—a social, mobile, and cloud-based communications platform for the future.[5] Together, they represent a tremendous opportunity for the enterprise to increase consumer engagement, break down information silos, and deliver highly targeted solutions at a lower cost.

The accessibility of mobile computing is a key influencer in digital disruption. The mobile industry is the fastest growing industry on the planet.[6] The personal computer has fallen of the cliff as smartphones and tablets have risen in popularity.[7]

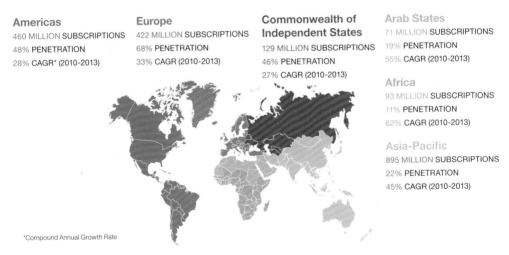

Americas
460 MILLION SUBSCRIPTIONS
48% PENETRATION
28% CAGR* (2010-2013)

Europe
422 MILLION SUBSCRIPTIONS
68% PENETRATION
33% CAGR (2010-2013)

Commonwealth of Independent States
129 MILLION SUBSCRIPTIONS
46% PENETRATION
27% CAGR (2010-2013)

Arab States
71 MILLION SUBSCRIPTIONS
19% PENETRATION
55% CAGR (2010-2013)

Africa
93 MILLION SUBSCRIPTIONS
11% PENETRATION
82% CAGR (2010-2013)

Asia-Pacific
895 MILLION SUBSCRIPTIONS
22% PENETRATION
45% CAGR (2010-2013)

*Compound Annual Growth Rate

FIGURE 1.5: Almost as Many Mobile Subscriptions as People in the World[8]

[5] "Transform Your Business With the Nexus of Force", Gartner, Inc., February, 2014.

[6] "Major Mobile Trends Show Global Mobile Industry is now the Fastest Growing Market in the World", MobileMarketingWatch.com, http://www.mobilemarketingwatch.com/major-mobile-trends-show-global-mobile-industry-is-now-thefastest-growing-market-in-the-world-16840/ (accessed June 2013).

[7] Chetan Sharma,"2013 Mobile Industry Predictions Survey", Chetan Sharma Consulting, January 2013, http://www.chetansharma.com/MobilePredictions2013.htm (accessed May 2013).

[8] Ibid.

Currently, there are almost as many mobile subscriptions as there are people in the world, creating expectations around the ability to immediately access and share information.[9] In total, 91 percent of all people on the planet have a mobile phone and 50 percent of these people used mobile as their primary Internet source.[10] In the very near future, there will be more people accessing the Internet on mobile devices than on personal computers.[11]

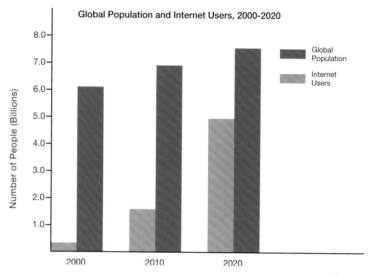

FIGURE 1.6: Increasing Internet Usage

Based on the above statistics, Internet usage will rise proportionally as the adoption of mobile devices increases. In 2000, there were 360 million Internet users; in 2010, there were 1.7 billion users; and by the year 2020 the number is expected to jump to 5 billion users.[12] With enhanced communications, the world is becoming a smaller place. Hyper-mobile connectivity is already affordable and widespread.

[9] ITU, "The World in 2013: ICT Facts and Figures" International Telecommunication Union, http://www.itu.int/en/ITU-D/Statistics/Pages/facts/default.aspx (accessed December 2013).

[10] "Infographic: 2013 Mobile Growth Statistics", Digital Buzz Blog, Tuesday Oct 1, 2013, http://www.digitalbuzzblog.com/infographic-2013-mobile-growth-statistics/ (accessed February, 2014).

[11] Frank Gens, IDC Predictions 2013: Competing on the 3rd Platform," IDC, 2012, http://www.idc.com/research/Predictions13/downloadable/238044.pdf (accessed February 2014).

[12] "Internet use reaches 5 billion worldwide", Future Timeline.net, http://www.futuretimeline.net/21stcentury/2020.htm#internet-2020 (accessed March 2014).

The growth in Internet users will result in more people gathering, transmitting, and exchanging information online. The Internet will continue to grow as a channel for distribution, revamping value chains in many industries. In the year 2020, the delivery of software, video, audio, games, and other media content will be almost entirely digital. The transformation from analog to digital is well underway, as email and texting render the postal industry obsolete; newspapers are replaced by online websites and user-generated content; and record labels and outlets are subverted by the artists distributing music themselves and online retailers like Apple iTunes. In 2020, further breakthroughs in wireless network innovation will drive economic and societal growth in entirely new ways.

Zero-Distance Connectivity

The future of the Internet is being fueled by advances in connectivity and capacity. In 2020, 5G wireless networks will support 1,000-fold gains in capacity, connections for at least 100 billion devices, a 10-gigabyte capacity, and an end-user experience based on extremely low latency and fast response times. Emerging sometime between 2020 and 2030, these networks will provide zero-distance connectivity between people and connected machines.[13]

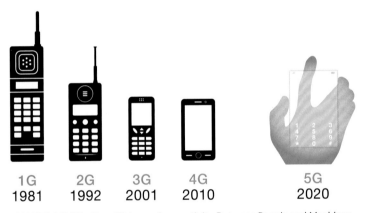

1G 1981 2G 1992 3G 2001 4G 2010 5G 2020

FIGURE 1.7: 5G - Zero Distance Connectivity Between People and Machines

[13] "5G: A Technology Vision", Huawei Technologies Co., Ltd., 2013.

The boundaries between technology and people will blur; connections between users and the network will surpass the speed of thought. Texting by thought will replace texting by smartphone. When combined with breakthroughs in the quantum teleportation of information (which are already taking place[14]), the instant transfer of information will enhance machine-to-machine communications and other technologies. As society becomes more connected, mobile devices will become further ingrained in the way we work and live our daily lives. Within the next decade, mobile apps will have the potential to connect to anything at any time—people, networks, appliances, cars, and much more to help society build increasingly "smart" cities. As the Internet becomes the dominant platform for many aspects of our lives, we will spend more time in the cloud.

Moving to the Cloud

The cloud has become a defining technology for the 21st century. In the future, large-scale cloud architectures will allow Internet service to be delivered at unprecedented speeds to meet demands for mobile traffic, connectivity, security, and mobile app development.

The term "the cloud" is a metaphor that was inspired by the cloud symbol used to represent the Internet in flow charts and diagrams. It represents an abstraction of the underlying structure of the Internet (as shown in the illustration below). Examples of cloud services include everything from basic Google® email to sophisticated business process software that is run remotely to reduce costs and enhance flexibility. Cloud computing describes the disruptive transformation of IT toward a service-based model, driven by economic, technological and cultural conditions.[15]

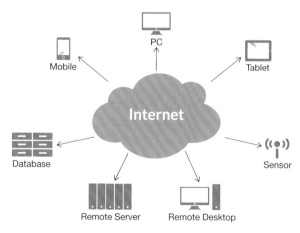

FIGURE 1.8: The Cloud

[14] James Vincent, *"Scientists achieve quantum teleportation breakthrough that could prove Einstein wrong"*, The Independent, May 30, 2014, *http://www.independent.co.uk/news/science/scientists-achieve-quantum-teleportation-breakthrough-that-could-prove-einstein-wrong-9462053.html* (accessed July 2014).

[15] Simon Wardley, *Cloud Computing - Why IT Matters*, YouTube, 2009.

Cloud services combine thousands of computers and storage networks, or public mainframes, into server farms. The power of the cloud lies in this immense server infrastructure. Facebook® has one of the most trafficked websites and runs thousands of databases in one of the largest server installations in the world. Google owns over one million servers spread across the globe to support its services. All major software vendors run server farms. These data centers represent the largest collection of information and computer resources in the world and number well over 500,000 (occupying roughly 5,955 football fields placed side by side).[16] Some of these data centers are so large they require their own power generators. Cloud computing represents the commercialization of these data center developments.

A key benefit—and the premise for how cloud computing has revolutionized IT—is the ability to "rent" computing services from a third-party provider, rather than owning and maintaining the physical infrastructure. Hardware or software resources are consumed as a service and, unless the service is free, consumers pay only for the resources they use or are billed on a subscription basis. Cloud computing is analogous to how traditional utility services like hydro are consumed as a metered, pay-as-you-go service. By outsourcing infrastructure or applications to the cloud, organization can focus on lowering their total cost of ownership by making fixed costs variable.

With the increasing adoption of mobile computing devices and improvements in connectivity, the potential for cloud-related technologies is immense. The cloud gives organizations the ability to respond quickly and nimbly to market opportunities and change because they are not hindered by costly and outdated legacy systems. The cloud concept can also make existing systems of information even more powerful. For example, big data is based on the premise that data in high volumes can't be assessed without the use of powerful software and computing systems. Organizations may use the cloud to access larger data sets and combine these data sets with their own enterprise information for improved insights, supporting a temporary need for increased computing power to analyze the data in the cloud. This allows for the much needed agility and adaptability, both of which are defining characteristics of digital business, discussed in greater detail in Chapter 2. The cloud is a fundamental enabler of digital disruption and a key contributor to the evolution of the Internet.

[16] Rich Millar, "How Many Data Centers? Emerson Says 500,000", December, 2011, http://www.datacenterknowledge.com/archives/2011/12/14/how-many-data-centers-emerson-says-500000/ (Accessed May, 2014).

The Internet of Everything

The IoT has been identified as the next phase in the evolution of the Internet. As the world's new digital nervous system, the IoT brings together wireless technologies, Micro-Electromechanical Systems (MEMS) and Internet technology to connect many disparate machines to exchange information.[17]

Machine-to-machine (M2M) technologies like Radio Frequency Identification (RFID) tags, sensors, video cameras, GPS, and smart cards are the primary enablers of the IoT. They capture data on the identity, status, condition, and location of physical assets. By monitoring devices attached to people, animals, or objects, the IoT automatically exchanges information over a network without requiring human-to-human or human-to-computer interaction. Instead, data exchange is based on M2M communications between the personal identifiers and the systems receiving the data via the Internet.

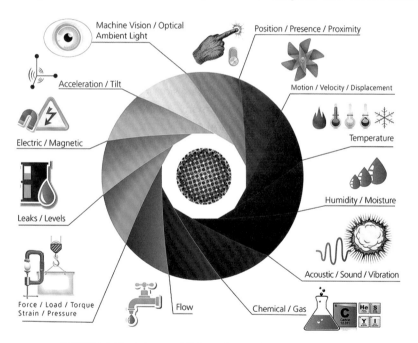

FIGURE 1.9: The Internet of Things - Connecting Devices, Sensors, RFID tags, Meters, and Smart Appliances[18]

---

[17] "What Exactly Is The "Internet of Things"?" Infographic, Harbour Research and Postscapes, http://postscapes.com/what-exactly-is-the-internet-of-things-infographic (accessed March 2014).

[18] Ibid.

The IoT will redefine the context of interactions by adding connectivity to everything from mobile devices, traditional appliances, and wearable computing. The IoT is finding its way into U.S. households, as 69 percent of consumers plan to buy a network-connected device for their home within the next five years.[19] By 2020, the number of connected devices will range from as little as three times the world's population (or roughly 25 billion) to as many as 1 trillion devices (120 times the population)—each having its own Internet Protocol (IP) address.[20]

Measuring the impact of the IoT is difficult, but its potential is enormous. Examples of the IoT are available today in the form of wearable devices like fitness sensors and smartwatches, implanted heart monitors, microchips in pets, and cars with built-in sensors. Beyond individuals, corporations and governments are making use of sensor-based technologies to improve inventory control or energy management through things like smart grids. The IoT makes sensors, machines, and devices much more useful or "smart" by connecting them to a network.

A Smart Future

In accordance with Moore's Law, smart machines are evolving at breakneck speed. Machines have already evolved from automating simple tasks to becoming self-learning, Artificial Intelligence (AI) systems. One of many AI projects in development, "Baby X" is a psychobiological simulation of an infant that learns, responds, and interacts in real time.[21] As early as 2017, it is believed that 10 percent of computers will be learning rather than processing.[22] Based on more powerful microprocessors, the creation of a variety of sensors and improved analytics, smart systems will become "smarter" and more applicable to our daily lives.

By 2024, 10 percent of activities that can be harmful to humans will require the use of mandatory smart systems.[23] In the transportation industry, smart systems like anti-lock braking systems, air bags, and crash avoidance systems are standard features that are fully automated. Automatic pilots and landing systems have been used for decades. While the presence of a human pilot is still preferred in planes, fully automated transit systems are common and autonomous vehicles are finding their way onto our roads and highways.

---

[19] "The Internet of Things: The Future of Consumer Adoption", Acquity Group, Accenture Interactive, 2014.

[20] "Gartner Says the Internet of Things Installed Base Will Grow to 26 Billion Units By 2020", Gartner Inc., December 12, 2013.

[21] Pam Baker, "BabyX reads its first words—artificial intelligence is growing up", FierceBigData, Aug 7, 2014, http://www.fiercebigdata.com/story/babyx-reads-its-first-words-artificial-intelligence-growing/2014-08-27 (accessed Aug 2014).

[22] Daryl C. Plummer et al, "Gartner Top Predictions 2014: Plan for a Disruptive, but Constructive Future", Gartner, Inc., October 7, 2013.

[23] Ibid.

Google has been working on developing a driverless car. Based on a vision of the future and powered by software called Google Chauffeur®, robotic cars can drive more quickly, efficiently, and safely, with more precise reflexes than humans and the potential to eliminate accidents and traffic congestion. While the car is not for sale, it can currently be seen driving down the streets of Mountain View, California. Other recent smart innovations include a streetlight system that improves traffic flow and a smart highway that eliminates the need for streetlights. The latter includes temperature sensors that light up the highway with symbols to describe road conditions and induction coils under lanes to charge electric cars as they drive over top.[24]

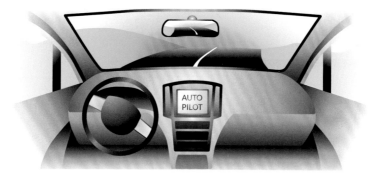

FIGURE 1.10: The Driverless Car

In 2020, the efficient operation of smart cities will be reliant on the IoT, with sensors measuring traffic flow, energy use, pollution, and the transit system to optimize performance. A municipal water system connected to the Internet can monitor pressure, wear, and leakages, and trash containers can alert waste removal when service is required. In the feature below, the City of Barcelona has a digital strategy in place to evolve itself into the smart city of the future.

[24] Smart Highway, *http://www.studioroosegaarde.net/project/smart-highway/stories/#804* (accessed May 2014).

The City of Barcelona

The solution, based on the principles of mobility, smart cities and administration, information systems and innovation, supports 150 portals with over 4 million user visits and more than 65 million pages generated each month.

FIGURE 1.11: An Innovative Mobile Identification System

The City of Barcelona is the capital of Catalonia, the second largest city in Spain, and the recognized European Capital of "Innovation 2014"—an award given by the European Commission for the City's use of new technologies to bring it closer to over a million and a half citizens. Fulfilling its vision of transformation into a smart city, the municipal government is relying on mobile- and cloud-based digital solutions to facilitate citizen engagement with administrative processes and city services.

The goals of implementing a digital strategy are clear: to make data and services available from any device and any location as a means to improve the quality of life for all citizens. A first step toward achieving this was making City Council and other data available in digital format, while promoting the reuse of this information to stimulate economic growth through opportunities for innovation. To standardize its information, the City needed to consolidate its infrastructure based on interoperable and open standards, and decommission its legacy systems. The City opted to migrate its solutions to the cloud.

The City of Barcelona is an example of a smart city. It is using digital solutions to transform itself into a connected hub for all city stakeholders to deliver quality services, improve its performance, and stimulate opportunities for economic development. The City markets itself as the mobile world capital, with 100 percent mobile access to services that bring its citizens closer to the city. Services are "one tap away" and include an innovative, web-based mobile identification system, mobileID, supported by a secure mobile registry of users. This system enables citizens to log in to access government services using their mobile device. As a result, the City of Barcelona has been able to meet citizens' needs, while improving efficiency and productivity through the digitization and automation of internal processes.

In the future, many of our everyday appliances will have the ability to self-monitor and communicate with a network—from coffee machines that send notifications when coffee is made to washers and driers that automatically upgrade based on online updates to refrigerators that place grocery orders online according to inventory.

While AI is being embedded into household appliances, nanobots are examples of AI that can be embedded into living organisms on a microscopic scale. Nanobots are machines the size of a nanometer that can be used for everything from repairing space satellites to killing cancerous cells when injected into the bloodstream.

While people are benefiting from pacemakers, artificial hearts, and hearing aids, breakthroughs in bioelectronics can make changes at the intracellular level to alter human biological structure. In the future, nanobots will be able to sense stimuli, perform complex calculations, communicate, and collaborate. In theory, nanobots can be programed to build proteins and microprocessors—and even more nanobots (through auto-replication) enabling a small group of nanobots to grow into a swarm to tackle complex projects and diseases.

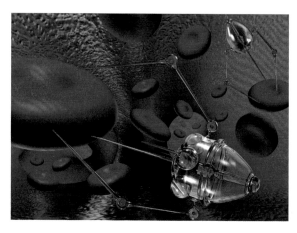

FIGURE 1.12: A Swarm of Nanobots

As nanobots move closer to becoming a reality, electronics are becoming increasingly more intelligent and human-like. In the year 2020, our devices will have the ability to listen to us (through voice recognition software), act as our eyes to monitor aspects of our lives, visually and otherwise, and respond to our touch. Touch screens have already revolutionized how we interact with our devices; wearable devices will take interaction to a new level.

You Are What You Wear

In the future, wearable technology will give marketers more opportunities to engage with consumers to deliver targeted products and services where and when they need them. From pedometers to wristband monitors to cameras stitched into clothing—as technologies that allow users to stay connected and hands-free, wearable devices are moving into mainstream society. Led by health and fitness markets, wearables are contributing to the trend of the "quantified self"—or self-knowledge gained through self-tracking with technology.

One of the most talked-about forms of wearables is Google Glass®. Positioned as "smart eyewear", Google Glass presents users with an optical computer embedded into a pair of glasses that can be controlled using voice commands. These devices (priced at U.S. $1,500 a pair) provide users with a seamless experience and will effect changes across industries with myriad applications. For example, field workers will be able to transmit videos, access diagnostic data, and make updates on location. The New York Police Department is already experimenting with the Google Glass technology and Dubai law enforcement plans to use them to spot speeding motorists and identify stolen cars.[25]

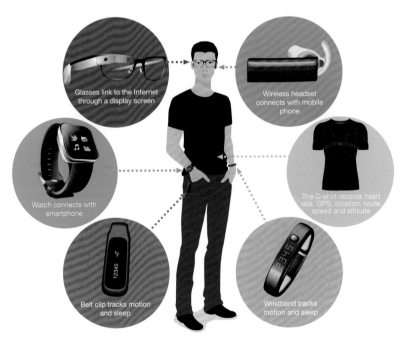

Glasses link to the Internet through a display screen

Wireless headset connects with mobile phone

Watch connects with smartphone

The D-shirt records heart rate, GPS, location, route, speed and altitude

Belt clip tracks motion and sleep

Wristband tracks motion and sleep

FIGURE 1.13: Wearable Technology

[25] *"Dubai cops may try Google Glass to catch speeders"*, rt.com, May 2014, http://rt.com/news/160552-dubai-cops-google-glass/ (Accessed May 2014).

By 2020, wearable technologies will become more sophisticated and the combined market for wearable devices will exceed US $12 billion.[26] By this time, the IoT will be integrating data, people, and processes in new and varying ways, resulting in the creation of new products and services. Since industries will be affected by the consolidation of information from diverse systems, the ability to tap into the broad network created by the IoT will be critical to the enterprise in 2020.

Connecting smart objects to the Internet gives them the ability to "sense" the environment, provide user context, and deliver much more personalized services. As devices interact with each other, connect with people via wearable tech, and generate vast amounts of data, the possibilities to engage and improve products and services seem limitless. Along with the IoT and wearable technologies, 3-D printing will further disrupt society and initiate a digital industrial revolution. Business leaders will have to plan strategically in the context of this revolution as it will affect consumers, businesses, industries, and even governments.

3-D Printing

In his recent State of the Union Address, U.S. President Barack Obama ushered in the digital industrial revolution with the following statement: "3-D printing has the potential to revolutionize the way we make almost everything. We must ensure that the next industrial revolution in manufacturing will happen in America. We can get that done."[27]

FIGURE 1.14: MakerBot's Thing-O-Matic® 3-D Printer[28]

[26] Daryl C. Plummer et al, "Gartner Top Predictions 2014: Plan for a Disruptive, but Constructive Future", Gartner, Inc., October 7, 2013.

[27] "MakerBot and Partners Are Leading the Charge to Crowd Source A MakerBot Desktop 3D Printer in Every School in America", BusinessWire, November 12, 2014, http://www.marketwatch.com/story/makerbot-and-partners-are-leading-the-charge-to-crowd-source-a-makerbot-desktop-3d-printer-in-every-school-in-america-2013-11-12 (accessed July 2014).

[28] MakerBot: http://www.makerbot.com/blog/2010/09/25/announcing-makerbots-new-3d-printer-the-thing-o-matic/ (accessed September 2014).

Innovations in this field are worthy of mention by the U.S. President because 3-D printing, 3-D manufacturing, and 3-D production will radically transform the nature of business and the structure of entire industries. Three-dimensional printing is a different kind of disruption because it produces physical objects from digital sources or designs.

Here's how 3-D printers work: they lay down substances in layers to create an object. Like a dot-matrix printer, the printer head moves back and forth printing out layers until the object is complete. Although the most common 3-D printers print in plastic, they can also be 3-D printed in 200 different materials, including glass, steel, bronze, gold, titanium, cake frosting, and chocolate. As an example of additive manufacturing, this process contrasts with subtractive manufacturing, in which materials are removed to create an object.

As with early laser printers, 3-D printing is expensive and hard to use, but (according to Moore's Law) they will soon be more powerful and affordable. Three-dimensional printing is already revolutionizing production in a handful of industries, most notably in health care: some prosthetics and even entire human organs are being 3-D printed (also known as bio-printing). Toys, jewelry, makeup, machine parts, automobile accessories, and engine parts have been 3-D printed. American designers at Local Motors are working on producing a 3-D printed car in just one day. In Holland, architects have begun construction on the first full-sized 3-D-printed house (with assembly complete in three years) and in China, ten full-sized houses were 3-D printed in a single day at a cost of less than US $5,000 per house. Inroads are even being made in the food industry as the first 3-D printed hamburger was created in England.[29]

At the moment, 3-D printers are expensive and unreliable, but in the next few years, the market will be poised for a mainstream 3-D printer. Currently, there are more than 23,000 3-D printers on the global market[30] and the industry is forecasted to grow to more than US $5.7 billion by 2017.[31] The number of 3-D printer manufacturers is increasing based on the success of MakerBot, Formlabs® and 3Doodler®. Viewed as a strategic technology that will revolutionize manufacturing around the world, governments are financially backing 3-D printing research and product development.

As a society, however, we are still fairly dependent on products that are mass-produced on an assembly-line. Based on cost, it is far cheaper to buy goods produced by traditional subtractive technology. And while 3-D manufacturing is making inroads into automotive, transportation, aerospace and defense, consumer, education, architecture, and health care, barriers to entry are based on copyright, intellectual property, and ethical issues.

---

[29] Linda Federico-O'Murchu, *"How 3D Printing Will Radically Change the World"* CNBC, May 2014. *http://www.cnbc.com/ id/101638702* (accessed May 2014).

[30] Garry Evans, *"Disruptive Technologies: Winners and losers from game changing innovation"*, HSBC Global Research, October 2013.

[31] *"Gartner Top Predictions 2014: Plan for a Disruptive but Constructive Future"*, October 7, 2013.

If objects can be scanned and printed using both a 3-D scanner (that creates images of an object using lights or lasers and turns this into a 3-D image) and a 3-D printer, the designs of objects can be easily copied and distributed. Ironically, the sources of technological innovation—open source, crowdsourcing, rapid prototyping—make intellectual property theft using 3-D printers easier to accomplish. With reduced manufacturing costs, intellectual property thieves will be able to produce knock-offs at a discount. Unsuspecting consumers could be at risk of poor performing and non-compliant or dangerous products.

FIGURE 1.15: 3-D Printed Prosthetic Hand

Even more controversial than intellectual property theft is the concept of bio-printing, or the ability of 3-D printers to print living tissues and organs. The 3-D printer is part of a system that includes medical imaging data and software that specifies the design of living tissue and organs to create an organ from an individual's own or another's cells. Once the cells are in place, they can grow into an organ. Experiments with bladders and kidneys have already been successful. Researchers at Hangzhou Dianzi University in China printed a kidney that lasted four months. Earlier in 2013, a two-year-old girl in the U.S. received a windpipe "printed" using her own stem cells.[32]

While bio-printing has lofty goals, there is a potentially negative side to these developments. Who will be eligible for bio-prints? And who will regulate their production? The realities behind being able to produce an organ for someone who needs one will help overcome the fears of a revolutionary new technology and the manufacturing industry's unwillingness to adopt it. At its most promising potential, 3-D printing expands opportunity to both consumers and manufacturers and increases sustainability based on reduced inventory, waste, cost, and carbon footprint.

---

[32] *"Young Girl Receives Lifesaving Windpipe Transplant Made From Her Stem Cells"*, Oristem, May 2013, *http://www.oristem.com/uk/en/index.php/component/story/?view=storyview&Itemid=133&article_id=340#.U3yqXfldVJM* (accessed May 2014).

Another key benefit of 3-D printing is that, as a desktop fabrication tool, it allows for rapid prototyping—the kind that fuels mass innovation and makes micro or desktop manufacturing a reality. The industrial playing field is leveled as the supply chain merges production with supply, and any business or individual can upload files to have their invention made or even make it themselves with a 3-D printer.

This allows for innovation cycles to move into hyper-drive. Objects can be created more quickly, less expensively, and with little complexity. Designers do not even have to be aware of the traditional manufacturing process for concept creation, which simplifies feasibility testing. Another benefit of 3-D manufacturing is the ability to produce goods for the Long Tail and serve a niche market. Designers can bypass the manufacturing process. Favoring customization, 3-D printing provides a choice for consumers between mass-produced goods and highly personalized ones. The Internet laid the foundations for this digital industrial revolution by opening up distribution and making a global marketplace available online.

Digital Changes Everything

Whether we like it or not, digital is now a part of everything we do—as individuals, as business leaders, and as a society. Digital disruptions are converging and impacting how we live our lives. All of these new technologies are steadily becoming extensions of ourselves as the lines blur between our hard drives and our brains. Like some futuristic movie, we are outsourcing our memories, communications, and more to these technologies. As we continue to accessorize ourselves with digital capabilities and assets, by 2020, the network effect will be diffusive.

The convergence of digital technologies is accelerating the pace of innovation and heralding a new digital industrial age. Automation and mass production are being replaced by disruptive technologies. Changes are being driven by a new economy that resembles the web: it is open, distributed, and highly entrepreneurial. To succeed in this nebulous digital environment, organizations will need to determine the value of these new disruptive technologies and how they can expand their abilities to compete in their markets.

The new digital reality extends beyond the firewall (and IT departments) to mobile devices, social media, smart machines, and the IoT. The old business models no longer apply. Instead, organizations need to adopt a digital business strategy to satisfy their digital customers, and they will have to do this quickly to lead their markets and remain competitive.

Based on the progress of the past and the present rate of change, how will digital technology transform business models to meet the needs of the workplace, the supply chain, and marketing channels in the future? What will the enterprise look like in 2020? The following chapter examines this in greater detail.

CHAPTER 2

DIGITAL BUSINESS

CHAPTER 2
Digital Business

"No business can afford to ignore or underplay the impact of technology-driven disruptions that are transforming what it means to be a business in a digital world."[1]

Disruptive innovations are initiating seismic shifts in our society. They are ushering in new ways of living, working, and conducting business. We are currently in the midst of this transformation but, by the year 2020, all of the major operating functions of the enterprise will be digital. Organizations will need to digitize every process and re-configure their businesses to ensure competitiveness and effectiveness. But what exactly is a digital business? What enables it? What are its primary characteristics? In this chapter, we explore what it means to be a successful digital business in a digital-first world.

FIGURE 2.1: A Traditional Linear Value Chain

A digital business is more than just a business with digital products that are distributed electronically: it's a business in which digital technology is both pervasive and central to its overall success. A digital business is created using digital assets and/or capabilities, involving digital products, services and customer experiences, and is conducted through digital channels and communities.[2] In a digital business, the majority of processes are digitized. This means that all along the value chain—from the creation of products and services to their consumption—employees, consumers, partners, and processes are reliant on digital technology for easy access to information, constant connectivity, and immediacy of insight.

A digital business is characterized by an open, flexible value chain. In the transition to a digital business, organizations need to re-envision their business not as a standalone entity with a linear value chain (as illustrated in Figure 2.1), but as part of an extended enterprise ecosystem of suppliers from which customers assemble products and services according to their needs (Figure 2.2). Organizations need to participate in these ecosystems to deliver value to customers.[3]

[1] *"Gartner Top Predictions 2014: Plan for a Disruptive, but Constructive Future"*, Gartner, Inc., October 7, 2013.

[2] Ibid.

[3] Nigel Fenwick and Martin Gill, *"The Future of Business Is Digital"*, Forrester Research, March 10, 2014.

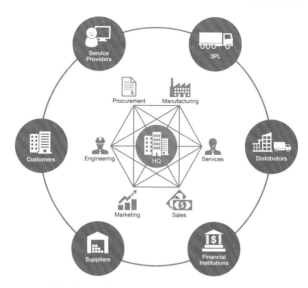

FIGURE 2.2: The Extended Enterprise Ecosystem

By positioning products and services in the context of the customer's value system, a digital business can grow its capabilities, leverage the capabilities of others, and open up new revenue streams. As part of a larger ecosystem, companies are more equipped to quickly pivot their operations to add customization or deliver new products to satisfy consumer need. They can scale their manufacturing capacity and shift geographies as needed to fill a specific order. In the future, these ecosystems will consist of low-cost suppliers and virtual manufacturers, be global in nature, and serve niche industries that span nations. Innovation will occur in hyper-drive, propelled forward by digital product development and marketing.

Digital technologies enable new business models that are dynamic, flexible, and deliver value to both businesses and customers. Before we examine how the enterprise can reinvent itself, it would be helpful to examine the circumstances that are driving the enterprise toward digital transformation.

The Drivers of Digital Transformation

The previous chapter highlighted the rapid pace of digitalization and how this wave of digital disruption is stronger and faster than technology disruptions of the past. Business leaders around the globe anticipate the rapid and transformational impact of digital technologies on their businesses. A 2014 survey of 1,243 global business executives found that 93 percent believe digital will disrupt their business within the next 12 months[4]. And they expect that the change to be radical and complete—reaching all parts of the organization.

[4] Nigel Fenwick and Martin Gill, *"The Future of Business Is Digital"*, Forrester Research, March 10, 2014.

FIGURE 2.3: Drivers of Digital Transformation[5]

Digital technologies are a major driver of business strategy. "From big data to cloud computing, executives see digital technologies as transforming business—more than half (52 percent) see them as driving either a *complete transformation* or *significant change*."[6] To empower the digital enterprise, business leaders need to embrace future trends in technology.

In 2020, the enterprise will either evolve or it will get disrupted. Several important factors are at work accelerating the adoption of digital technologies and, in particular, driving the transformation of businesses into digital businesses. These include:

- The nature of digital technology
- Generation Z and their new expectations for the workplace
- Demands of the digital customer
- Growing requirements for operational agility
- Continued globalization
- Regulatory pressures and the need for information security and governance

[5] Connie Moore, "*The Process-Driven Business of 2020*", Forrester Research, April 16, 2012.

[6] Accenture, "*CEO Briefing 2014*", Global Agenda, 2014.

The Nature of Digital Technology

Digital technologies enable new businesses models that are dynamic, flexible, and deliver value to both businesses and customers. Central to digital transformation is the ability to facilitate direct, peer-to-peer communication, collaboration, and sharing, without requiring an intermediary. This ability is already reshaping business as we know it. By providing direct, unrestricted access to information, knowledge, and resources, digital technologies empower individuals in ways not previously possible or even imaginable. Anyone with a web-enabled device can connect to a global network of expertise. They can discover individuals with common interests and goals. They can share ideas, collaborate, and innovate. They can band together and have their voice heard, counted, and taken seriously by those in positions of influence. And they can access new channels for manufacturing, marketing, and selling, and work with business partners located anywhere in the world.

As individuals are empowered with new ways of working, traditional channels—and those who control them—will hold less importance. An inventor, for example, no longer needs to license their product idea for pennies on the dollar to a manufacturer. They can prototype the product with three-dimensional (3-D) printing. They can "crowdfund" capital costs using the Internet (collecting small amounts of capital from family, friends, or members in their online community). They can market globally through inexpensive and accessible online channels, sell through a digital storefront, manufacture small batches or distribute digitally. All this can be done in ways that are faster and cheaper and deliver new value to the customer. In shifting power and influence away from traditional sources, digital technologies are introducing opportunity to the masses. Businesses must acknowledge, respond to, and allow digital technologies to transform their operations from the inside-out if they want to stay competitive and relevant in a digital-first world.

Generation Z

Generation Z is the first "digital" generation to enter the workforce. Having grown up with easy access to the Internet and persistent connectivity, they are technically savvy, earning them the nickname "digital natives".[7] Technology is central to the way Generation Z works and plays. They use digital technologies like social media to share information and interact with peers. Constant connectedness is a fact of life for this group, they function on the immediacy of real-time insight and action.

In 2020, Generation Z will expect to continue working in ways that are open, social, mobile, and flexible rather than fixed according to a hierarchical structure. They will want to use the same tools in the workplace that they use at home to communicate, collaborate, and share information. If the enterprise does not permit access to these digital tools, Generation Z will bring them inside the firewall, circumventing IT and established governance rules and policies. Not offering them as part of the IT infrastructure will not be an option.

[7] Generation Z: *http://en.wikipedia.org/wiki/Generation_Z* (accessed July, 2014).

As they enter the workforce, Generation Z will introduce the globalization of talent. While it works to support its existing workforce, the enterprise will need to change its business models and approach to recruiting, retaining, and motivating this workforce. The good news is that, if they are empowered, this highly agile workforce will help the enterprise on its journey to digital transformation. Chapter 6, "The Digital Workplace", provides a more detailed description of this demographic, their workplace requirements, and their transformational impact on business.

The Digital Customer

An increasingly connected consumer and the widespread adoption of digital technology has created the digital customer. Internet-based retail is growing globally at a rate of 19 percent year over year[8] and, as more consumers move online, they are using the Internet to discover products, gather and evaluate information, and engage the buyer online for purchasing and shipping. An increasing number of channels are offering customers convenience, flexibility, and choice. They expect immediate gratification and engaging experiences that satisfy. The digital enterprise will support the omni-channel delivery of goods and services to compete and satisfy their customers.

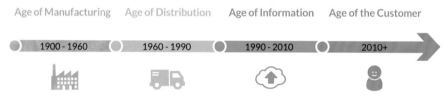

FIGURE 2.4: The Age of the Customer[9]

We have entered the "Age of the Customer"—an age in which digital technology has empowered the customer and shifted the balance of purchasing power from suppliers to customers.[10] Consumers now have the ability to extract price, quality, and service concessions from the world's most powerful brands.[11] What used to differentiate the enterprise—economies of scale, distribution strength, and brand—have faded in importance. In their place, customer obsession is what gives firms dominance and drives their competitive advantage.

For digital business, customer experience does not outweigh the need for operational excellence. In the feature below, Barrick Gold incorporates digital technology into their operations to prevent equipment failure, reduce production downtime, and maintain operational excellence.

---

[8] Daniel, Pallozzi, "Predictions for Retail 2020: A New Brick and Mortar Experience", December 4, 2013, http://www.thoughtworks.com/insights/blog/predictions-retail-2020-new-brick-and-mortar-experience (accessed July 2014).

[9] Laura Ramos, "Make B2B Marketing Thrive in the Age of the Customer", Forrester Research, May 21, 2013.

[10] Nigel Fenwick and Martin Gill, "The Future of Business is Digital", Forrester Research, March 10, 2014.

[11] George F. Colony and Peter Burris, "Technology Management in the Age of the Customer", Forrester Research, October 2013.

Barrick Gold

Barrick Gold Corporation is the world's leading gold mining company and a leading producer of copper. The company has its headquarters in Toronto, Canada, with mines and projects on five continents. Reflecting a focus on responsible, modern mining, Barrick has been listed on the Dow Jones Sustainability Index for seven consecutive years, and is ranked as the top performer in the mining industry category. Shares of the company are traded on the Toronto and New York stock exchanges under the symbol ABX.

Operational excellence is Barrick's goal in all areas of its business. In an interview with David Jamieson, Vice President, Information Management and Technology at Barrick, Mr. Jamieson discusses how digital technology plays a key role in helping Barrick achieve its industry-leading vision. What follows are excerpts from this interview.

FIGURE 2.5: Barrick Gold Corporation - Disciplined, Profitable Production

"Digital technology has greatly impacted our operations. With each year, our processes and operations are being enhanced with new capabilities, from equipment that is "smarter", sensors that enable tracking and monitoring, and systems that are tightly interconnected. Access to specific and real-time data about the performance of our mining processes gives us insights so we can make knowledgeable and timely operational decisions. For example, we can monitor in detail the health of engines in our haul trucks—these are rugged dump trucks specifically engineered for high-production mining. These trucks are core to our operations and preventing downtime is important. On-board diagnostics inform us when engine performance degrades so we can order in parts and proactively schedule maintenance. In addition we use high precision GPS to manage our shovels, trucks, loaders and drill rigs to ensure we can effectively manage the material that we mine and move. All of this digital information is helping us to improve our production efficiency and realize significant cost savings.

So, we have built a technology infrastructure that is rich in data—data that we use to make smart, real-time decisions to improve the performance of our mining operations and gain a competitive edge. This data, however, also presents us with significant challenges. There is a lot of data being generated around all aspects of our business and managing this data is probably our biggest challenge right now, given its exponential growth.

We generate significant volumes of data both on the operations side of our business, as well as on the license-to-operate side. Compliance with environmental and carbon footprint standards and our own internal policies are vitally important to us. Effective governance is a foundation of our performance and success as a publicly-traded mining company with sites around the world. Our obligations, expectations, and intentions are reinforced regularly at all levels of the company. For example, Barrick is committed to achieving a zero-incident work environment with a safety culture based on teamwork and safety leadership.

Information management is critical in communicating and enforcing policy. The company has implemented key safety programs and activities, including systems and policies, training for all employees, performance measurement, risk assessment processes, recognition programs for safety achievement, and a steady flow of information that keeps people focused on continuous safety improvement.

To ensure information from across our business is properly managed throughout its useful and defined lifecycle, we depend on an enterprise content management system. Information management transforms the value of information from "overload" to "asset". When information is effectively managed and captured, it becomes intellectual capital and knowledge. Enterprise content management enables information to support our business operations, rather than hinder them. As a result, our operations run smoothly and efficiently, we can demonstrate compliance, and we can better meet our strategic goals and business objectives. Digital technology and information management are two sides to the same coin. Together they give our business the capabilities and the discipline we need to grow and flourish in today's complex and competitive business environment.

The Need for Agility and Operational Excellence

Operational excellence is a key enabler of a superior customer experience. When a customer has an online experience that exceeds expectations but their product arrives damaged or late, this operational failure wipes out any previously positive experiences and negatively impacts brand and sales.

Operational excellence is becoming more important as digital customers have growing expectations for faster delivery of goods, increasing product personalization, and 24/7 engagement. In some cases, processes will need minor adjustments; in other cases, massive change is required. The net result, however, is the growing need for processes to be agile, adaptable, and able to rapidly respond to the needs of their markets.

A digital enterprise is process-driven and adopts technologies to make their processes highly adaptable to changing business needs, to support around-the-clock operations, and to automate the exchange of goods, communications, and commerce. We examine specific process management technologies in Chapter 5, "The Digital Supply Chain".

Globalization

Continued globalization is contributing to the shift toward digitization. Globalization is defined by Thomas Friedman, author of *The World is Flat*, as the interweaving of markets, technology, information systems, and telecommunications networks in a way that is shrinking the world from a size medium to a size small.[12]

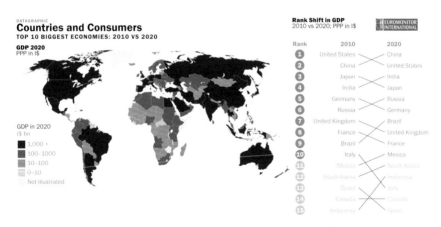

FIGURE 2.6: Top 10 Largest Economies In 2020 [13]

[12] Thomas L. Friedman, *"Most Overblown Fears: Globalization"*, Newsweek, 2010, *http://2010.newsweek.com/top-10/most-overblown-fears/globalization.html* (accessed July 2014).

[13] *"Top 10 largest economies in 2020"*, Euromonitor International from IMP, July 7, 2010, *http://blog.euromonitor.com/2010/07/special-report-top-10-largest-economies-in-2020.html* (accessed July 2014).

Globalization has accelerated dramatically over the last decade due to the falling price of computing power, which has made technology affordable and accessible and led to the widespread adoption of mobile and Internet-enabled devices. The result is an ever-more densely interconnected world. This interconnectedness enables businesses around the world to easily communicate, collaborate, and innovate as part of a global ecosystem. It also provides a more level playing field on which to compete for access to global resources, talent, and opportunity. In a digitally interconnected world, business barriers are lowered and location no longer determines business success.

As globalization continues to rise, we can expect to see capital, economic power, and influence shift from older economies in North America and Europe to emerging economies. By the year 2020, it is expected that Brazil, Russia, India, and China (collectively known as BRIC countries) will become dominant centers of economic influence.[14] They will have strong middle classes with significant purchasing power and will be sources of business innovation.

A digital business is well positioned to gain a presence in these markets, serve their customers, and collaborate with businesses located there. They can hire people in these locales and effectively integrate employees and business processes into a global infrastructure. They can leverage international tools, knowledge, and networks to influence local decision-making processes. The relationship between globalization and digital disruption is interdependent: each one fuels the growth of the other and both work together to shape digital business.

Regulatory Pressure

In 2020, growing regulatory and competitive pressures will require the digital enterprise to rethink and reprioritize their security and governance strategies for enterprise information. These requirements will be driven by new, global regulations, increasing amounts of Internet users and privacy-related issues, emerging sustainability metrics, open data, big data, and protection against Intellectual Property (IP) loss.

Global regulations are driving businesses to leverage technology both to declassify it and open it to a broader audience. On the opposite end of the spectrum, this technology must still provide rigorous security, classification, and controlled discovery. Regulatory pressure forces organizations to determine which data is worth protecting, since protecting all information is expensive and unnecessary. By 2017, governments and international organizations will adopt legislation around open data and the release of information that was previously unpublished. Instead of ensuring that all data is secure, the digital enterprise will focus on protecting only the information that requires it.[15]

---

[14] Jeanne C. Meister and Karie Willyerd, *"The 2020 Workplace"*, Harper Collins, May 11, 2010.

[15] *"Gartner Top Predictions 2014: Plan for a Disruptive, but Constructive Future"*, Gartner, Inc., October 7, 2013.

The Components of a 2020 Digital Business

As digital technologies transform business operations, all major components of the business will be impacted. The components of the 2020 digital business are already emerging and include the Digital Workplace, Digital Engagement, the Digital Supply Chain, and Digital Governance and Security. Let's examine them in further detail.

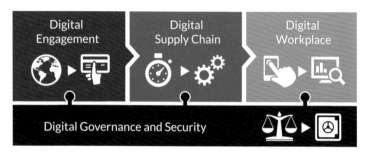

FIGURE 2.7: The Components of a Digital Business

The Digital Workplace

In the year 2020, our office will be everywhere; our team members will live halfway around the world. How, where, when, and for whom we work will be up to us—as long as we produce results.[16]

The continued trend toward globalization will greatly impact the 2020 workplace, with corporate headquarters and employment expected to continue shifting to developing countries, particularly BRIC nations. The resulting workplace will be dispersed and demographically diverse with employees on multiple continents, in multiple time zones.

The 2020 workforce will also be drawn from a pool that is smaller and older. In North America, Europe, and many parts of Asia, workforces are shrinking as birth rates decline. Germany, for example, will have a workforce in 2020 that is 20 percent smaller than it was in 2000 and a retired population that is 50 percent larger.[17] In the U.S., the population is expected to age with many older workers continuing to work after retirement. The growing number of aging workers means that many companies will be required, for the first time in modern society, to manage five generations in the workplace. The digital enterprise will have to create an environment that accommodates vastly different sets of values, beliefs, and expectations.

[16] Jeremy Rifkin, "The Zero Marginal Cost Society", Palgrave Macmillan Trade, April 1, 2014.

[17] Jeanne C. Meister and Karie Willyerd, "The 2020 Workplace", Harper Collins, May 11, 2010.

The changing demographics of the global workforce are related to a larger issue. Over the next five to ten years, smart machines and workplace automation will nudge people out of routine, repetitive tasks. Instead, people will focus on tacit, knowledge-based work, which is non-routine and relies on information for decision-making. Tacit jobs require a complex set of skills, such as problem-solving, judgment, listening, data analysis, relationship building, and collaborating and communicating with co-workers. These tacit jobs are predicted to grow two-and-a-half times faster than the transactional segment and will change the nature of the workforce.[18] While these jobs grow, there will be a shortage of workers with requisite skills. This skills shortage and a shrinking pool from which to draw from will result in organizations competing to attract workers with the right skill sets. Companies will need to create a work environment that is attractive and appealing to the 2020 knowledge worker.

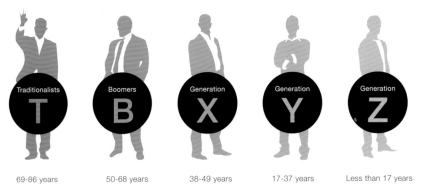

Traditionalists	Boomers	Generation X	Generation Y	Generation Z
69-86 years	50-68 years	38-49 years	17-37 years	Less than 17 years

FIGURE 2.8: Generation Z Constitutes Half of the Workforce

What will the 2020 workplace look like? We know it will be global and virtual with fewer on-site employees and leaner headquarter facilities. To facilitate this workforce, workplaces will depend on digital communications and collaboration in global conference calls, through instant-messaging and social communities, or by working on shared documents. Digital technology will accessorize and permeate the 2020 workplace to empower employees and drive competitive advantage.

[18] Jeremy Rifkin, *"The Zero Marginal Cost Society"*, Palgrave Macmillan Trade, April 1, 2014.

Digital Engagement

In the year 2020, digital will not just be a route to market; it will be the primary route to market. Businesses will connect directly with their customers through superior customer experiences—reaching and engaging customers at every touchpoint. Digital customers will bounce from task-to-task and device-to-device across relevant channels—discovering products in online articles and community discussions, researching competitors, downloading product specifications, purchasing through e-commerce sites, and engaging businesses through customer service portals. Each touchpoint provides an opportunity to strengthen and tighten customer relations. To be successful, the digital enterprise will need to provide its customers with a seamless buyer journey across many channels to deliver what they need, when and where they need it.[19]

FIGURE 2.9: Omni-Channel Marketing[20]

Omni-channel marketing will be used to digitally deliver a consistent brand experience across a complete ecosystem of partners. Consumers regard brands as a single entity and expect the same experience of its products and services, policies and processes, and personality, regardless of channel. They expect not only experiences appropriate for the channels being used, but also consistency across those experiences.[21] This is examined in more detail in Chapter 4, "Digital Engagement".

[19] Ron Rogowski, "The Unified Customer Experience Imperative", Forrester Research, May 7, 2013.

[20] Christopher Hall, "Digital Signage and the 'Store of the Future', Retail Customer Experience", Dec 10, 2013, http://www.retailcustomerexperience.com/articles/digital-signage-and-the-store-of-the-future/ (accessed July 2014).

[21] Stephen Powers and John R. Rymer, "Unify the Digital Experience Across Touchpoints", Forrester Research, August 22, 2012.

In 2020, digital businesses will use digital technologies to deepen engagement with customers. The key to engagement will be an organization's ability to access intelligence about consumers and use this information to target consumer need at each stage in the buying process.

Where does this customer intelligence come from? Customers in 2020 will leave "digital shadows" made up of data left by transactions and interactions on the Internet and provided by other connected devices and sensors. As people leave stronger digital shadows, marketers will use this information in real time to adapt content at a given touchpoint, delivering a highly personalized experience that is relevant and useful at that stage in the buying process.

Through consumer data and intelligence, the digital enterprise can better understand its consumers, define accurate segments, and tailor products and services to meet their needs. But insights are not only relevant for marketing. Insights from big data also enable the digital enterprise to measure supply chain logistics and produce outcomes that drive competitive advantage.

The Digital Supply Chain

In the year 2020, consumers will largely drive interactions with suppliers. They will expect greater customization of products, swift delivery of goods, and an experience that is smooth and seamless. To fulfill this vision, digital businesses will leverage information technology to support new levels of flexibility, operational excellence, and information exchange between supply chain partners, otherwise known as Business-to-Business (B2B) integration. In 2020, business networks will consist of vibrant and collaborative environments in which buyers, suppliers, and technology morph into a just-in-time, market-driven world requiring the right information, in the right form, in the right language, at the right time.[22] Digital business processes supported by a digital business network will be essential to success. Technologies like Smart Process Applications (SPAs) and Dynamic Case Management (DCM), when combined with approaches like distributed manufacturing and B2B integration, will bring flexibility, greater agility and efficiency, and customization to an extended enterprise ecosystem.

In a globalized, distributed manufacturing environment, companies will depend on B2B integration—technology and applications for the automated exchange of transactions (for example, purchase orders and invoices) between broad networks of global trading partners (such as suppliers, customers, and financial institutions). The 2020 B2B network will harness the cloud and offer full mobile access.

---

[22] Mike Lacobucci, *"Looking ahead to globalization 2020"*, MultiLingual Computing, http://www.moravia.com/files/download/Globalization2020_MultilingualComputing.pdf (accessed July 2014).

A final, notable force shaping the 2020 supply chain is the Internet of Things (IoT). The ability to tag products, for example, and track them (via the Internet) through various stages of the supply chain provides businesses with accurate, real-time information and insight into supply chain processes. Early stages of the IoT are in operation today in the industrial and commercial sectors. UPS, for example, embeds sensors into their 60,000 vehicles in the United States to monitor individual parts for signs of potential malfunction so they can replace them before a breakdown occurs.[23] In other industries, sensors record and communicate the availability of raw resources, inform the front office on current inventories in the warehouses, and troubleshoot dysfunctions on production lines. Sensors keep sales and marketing departments apprised of which items are being looked at, handled, and put back on shelves. They track the locations of products shipped to retailers and consumers and keep tabs on the amount of waste being recycled.

FIGURE 2.10: Distributed Manufacturing[24]

In the 2020 supply chain, the IoT will connect devices, information, processes, and people across business networks. Data from sensors, for example, will be used to recalibrate supply chain inventories, improve production and distribution processes, and initiate new business practices to increase efficiencies and productivity throughout the value chain.

[23] Jeremy Rifkin, "The Zero Marginal Cost Society", Palgrave Macmillan Trade, April 1, 2014.
[24] Ibid.

Digital Governance and Security

Every business and every department is subject to laws, rules, and regulations that require strict compliance to protect corporate assets. As digital technologies permeate the value chain, they are producing enormous amounts of data and content. With growing volumes of data and increasing opportunity for data theft, it will be crucial for organizations to have sound strategies and practices for information governance and security of private or sensitive information. As the enterprise reinvents itself, business leaders will need to articulate a digital strategy that balances innovation and growth with security and risk. Information management will increasingly leverage digital technology for compliance, good governance, and e-discovery. This is an important topic that will be discussed further in Chapter 7, "Digital Governance".

A Digital Strategy

In broad terms, digital business is billions of people, businesses, and devices communicating, collaborating, and transacting. Its potential is huge—from replacing paper and manual processes with software, to moving applications to the cloud to lower costs of ownership and increase agility, to applying analytics to deepen engagement with customers. But it involves more than just moving to an e-commerce model: it shakes business at its very core. It moves beyond digitizing every process to challenging old operational approaches and inventing new processes.

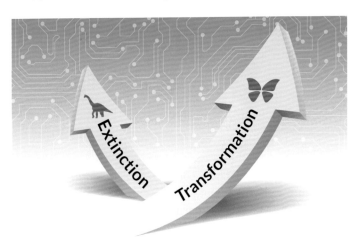

FIGURE 2.11: A Digital Strategy Is Fundamental to Transformation

Digital business upsets the status quo and operates using a flatter, socially-enabled business model. It promotes direct engagement between suppliers and consumers. In a traditional business model, it's the retailer, reseller, distributor, and shipping company that engages directly with the end consumer and, in some cases, provides after sales service and support. It's also common for market research and customer feedback to be gathered by third parties. In traditional businesses, the customer relationship is relegated to channels and third parties. This has been the nature of top-down hierarchical business models where customers purchase what manufacturers decide to produce.

What is required is a radical break from the past and the creation of entirely new business models with new expectations and new ways of working. Customers are already embracing digital technology and redirecting the value chain. Digital natives are entering the workplace and bringing new expectations for how they want to work. Value chains are being transformed, based on new business models and processes that are flexible, scalable, and better able to serve the customer.

Organizations will only be able to capitalize on this promise of opportunity and innovation if their focus remains fixed on the customer and finding the balance between marketing and operations. A digital business creates new revenue streams using digital resources. In order to do so successfully, they will need to develop a digital strategy to evolve their operations. The strategy should support a digital workforce and culture, infrastructure, operations, and engagement across the entire extended enterprise ecosystem.

Digital disruption will help evolve the enterprise into a digital business. However, to truly transform, organizations will need to govern and secure their information. As recent history has shown, information is the byproduct of digital disruption—*a lot of it*. In the future, everyone will participate in the new information economy as technology becomes more malleable and information is the means to production. Underlying the development of a digital strategy then must be an effective way to manage information to promote innovation and opportunity, while minimizing risk. This is discussed in the next chapter, "Information Is the New Currency".

CHAPTER 3

INFORMATION IS THE NEW CURRENCY

CHAPTER 3
Information is the New Currency

"Information assets are an instrument of innovation that can change the very nature of the business process, or even the business model. Business leaders are realizing that the increasing supply and availability of information can (and must) be used for competitive advantage, value generation, risk management/compliance, and transformation."[1]

Disruptive innovations in technology are challenging the established rules of business. What all these technologies have in common is that they enable a new way of using information. For the digital enterprise, information is no longer just a cost factor but rather the basis for growth and competitiveness.

The value of information is being increasingly regarded as an asset that must be managed. A recent study found that 95 percent of organizations correlate strong information management with business success.[2] Technology leaders of the past have been preoccupied with managing technology systems; today their focus is shifting to the strategic value of content. When managed effectively, it enhances performance, improves insight for better decision-making, increases customer satisfaction, and reduces risks of litigation and non-compliance.

In a digital-first economy, information is the new currency. It provides the means of production in a digital marketplace, facilitated by digital manufacturing and a distributed business network. In 2020, both organizations and individuals will monetize their data to create new revenue streams. One of the biggest business challenges related to digital transformation will be how to effectively manage growing volumes of information to optimize its value while reducing risk. But how can the enterprise unlock the potential of information without compromising productivity and security? This chapter examines this question in detail and introduces Enterprise Information Management (EIM) as the key transformative technology in a digital-first world.

How Much Data?

By all predictions, the amount of data we produce will continue to grow well into the future. In 2007, IDC produced the first in their annual series of *Digital Universe* reports. In it, the report revealed that we crossed a milestone: the amount of digital information that we created at this point in time had surpassed our ability to store it.[3]

---

[1] Douglas Laney and Andrew White, *"Agenda Overview for Information Innovation and Governance"*, 2014, Gartner, Inc., January 10, 2014

[2] Forbes Insights, *"Managing Information in the Enterprise: Perspectives for Business Leaders"*, Forbes Insight (2009), *http://fm.sap.com/data/UPLOAD/files/Managing%20Information%20in%20the%20Enterprise%20Perspectives%20for%20Business%20Leaders.pdf* (accessed 24 Oct. 2012).

[3] John Gantz, *"The Expanding Digital Universe"*, IDC: March, 2007.

The Digital Universe: **50-fold Growth** from the Beginning of 2010 to the End of 2020

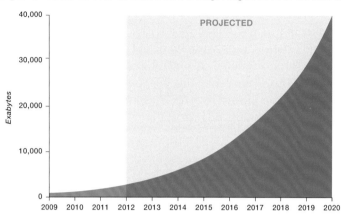

FIGURE 3.1: Growth of Information by Exabytes[4]

Over the last decade, the rate of information growth has increased exponentially. The five exabytes of information that existed globally in 2003 now represents the amount of content we create every two days. Consumers are adding to data volume as the ability to create and share information has accelerated by the number of people, devices, and sensors connected to networks. Multimedia is the most popular format of data shared on the Internet, with over 6 billion hours of video watched each month on YouTube—that's almost an hour for every person on Earth and 50 percent more than last year.[5] As far a social media is concerned, 1.31 billion active Facebook users per month share over 1 million links and 3 million messages[6] and upload 350 million photos a day.[7] Finally, the devices, sensors, Radio Frequency Identification (RFID) tags, meters, and smart appliances that make up the Internet of Things (IoT) are also contributing to the growth of data. According to analysts, there will be nearly 26 billion devices on the IoT by 2020.[8] That's a lot of potential information exchange. By 2020, the world will generate 50 times the amount of information it does currently and 75 times the number of "information containers", while the IT staff needed to manage it will grow fewer than 1.5 times.[9] As more people, processes and data interact, an information economy will emerge as the value of information increases—and outpace the skills required to manage it.

[4] John Gantz and David Reinsel, "*The Digital Universe in 2020: Big Data, Bigger Digital Shadows, and Biggest Growth in the Far East*", IDC: December, 2012.

[5] YouTube Statistics: *http://www.youtube.com/yt/press/statistics.html* (accessed January, 2014).

[6] Statistics Brain: *http://www.statisticbrain.com/facebook-statistics/* (accessed January, 2014).

[7] Craig Smith, "*By the Numbers: 64 Amazing Facebook User Statistics*", DMR, Digital Marketing Ramblings, December, 2013, *http://expandedramblings.com/index.php/by-the-numbers-17-amazing-facebook-stats/#.UtMD3_v5OXM* (accessed January, 2014).

[8] "*Gartner Says the Internet of Things Installed Base Will Grow to 26 Billion Units By 2020*" Gartner, Inc., December 12, 2013.

[9] John Gantz and David Reinsel, "*The Digital Universe in 2020: Big Data, Bigger Digital Shadows, and Biggest Growth in the Far East*", IDC, December, 2012.

These massive volumes of data are present in both the Public Web and the Deep Web. The Public Web refers to the portion of the web that can be indexed by search engines. With more than eight billion pages, the Public Web constitutes only four percent of the world's data. It is only the tip of the digital iceberg. Consumer sites like Google® and Facebook represent only a diminutive fraction in the ocean of information stored in modern systems. The rest of this information—96 percent of it—lives inside organizations, hidden behind firewalls. This is called the Deep Web. The Deep Web is what companies run their business on every day.

The Deep Web

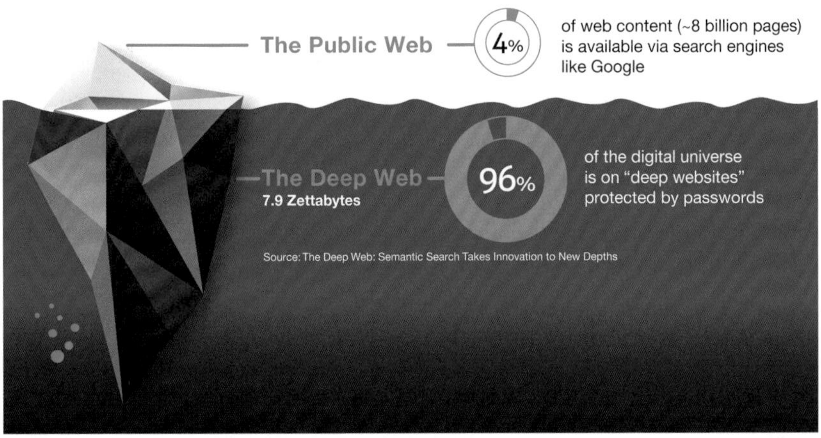

The Public Web — 4% of web content (~8 billion pages) is available via search engines like Google

The Deep Web — 96% of the digital universe is on "deep websites" protected by passwords
7.9 Zettabytes

Source: The Deep Web: Semantic Search Takes Innovation to New Depths

FIGURE 3.2: Deep Web Data Sources

Information as a Commodity

In every industry, organizations are collecting detailed amounts of information. The volume of content being created and stored by organizations is doubling every two years. Every day organizations face an increasing volume, velocity, and variety of information. For most organizations, this is not a trend but the reality of doing business. In other words, big data is not new: the Global 5000 have been working with extremely large data sets for decades, applying agents to scour information to better understand their customers, the way they transact with the company and how they influence other buyers in their peer group. This is the original big data.

What is new is the technology base that allows us to understand big data sets. These technologies enable big data sets to fit into non-mechanical memory, leverage more powerful processors and grid configurations, and have operations work 100 times or even 1,000 times faster than was previously possible. Massive amounts of value can be extracted from big data—from demographic behavior and product recommendations to buyer propensity models and geographical market uptake patterns.

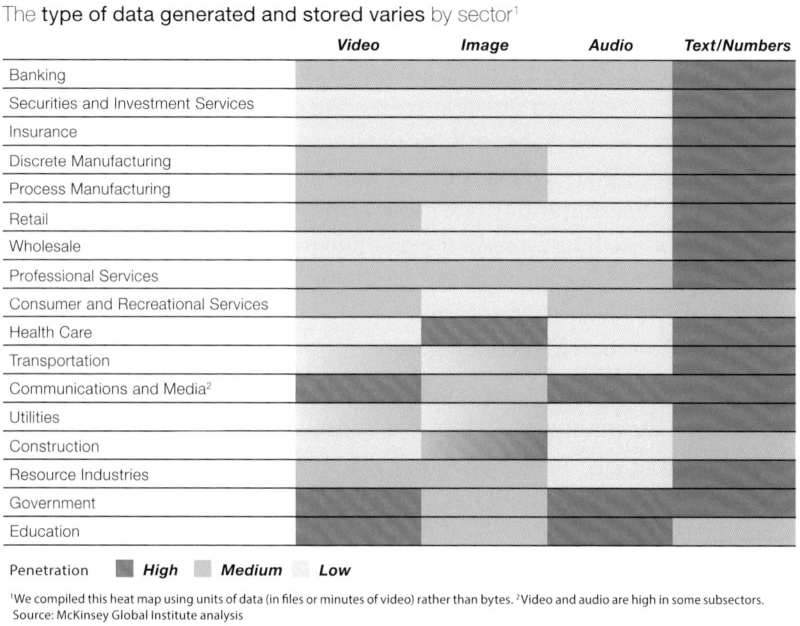

The **type of data generated and stored varies** by sector[1]

	Video	*Image*	*Audio*	*Text/Numbers*
Banking				
Securities and Investment Services				
Insurance				
Discrete Manufacturing				
Process Manufacturing				
Retail				
Wholesale				
Professional Services				
Consumer and Recreational Services				
Health Care				
Transportation				
Communications and Media[2]				
Utilities				
Construction				
Resource Industries				
Government				
Education				

Penetration ■ *High* ▨ *Medium* *Low*

[1]We compiled this heat map using units of data (in files or minutes of video) rather than bytes. [2]Video and audio are high in some subsectors.
Source: McKinsey Global Institute analysis

FIGURE 3.3: Types of Data Generated and Stored by Sector[10]

The promise of big data is the ability to make predictions based on it. Information can be viewed and analyzed, trends can be understood, and correlations can be plotted. The challenge, of course, is finding the value, especially when content volume is increasing. Even more challenging than this are the technologies that are creating new content without any human intervention, like sensors. In every organization, information is made up of combined system-generated and user-generated content, or structured and unstructured information.

[10] *"Big data: The next frontier for innovation, competition, and productivity"*, McKinsey Global Institute, McKinsey & Company, 2011.

Structured Vs. Unstructured Information

Structured information is data in fixed fields in a spreadsheet or a relational database that is housed in Enterprise Resource Management (ERP) systems. ERP tools share a common data model, covering operational end-to-end processes, such as those found in finance, human resources, distribution, manufacturing, service, and a supply chain. These processes depend on large volumes of data. Unstructured information is the conversation that forms around this data.

Unstructured information is pervasive. It is fueled by emerging Internet technologies and devices that provide the immediate access and exchange of information. Unstructured content is fragmented, mashed up, delivered across many channels, and accessible at any time in any place. It is unsystematic, difficult to dissect, and represents a staggering 80 percent of the enterprise's data today. It's the archived supplier invoice, expenses, contracts, receipts, presentations, faxes, memos, emails, social media, videos—the unstructured data of the business. As the complexity of this content increases, so does the need to understand, locate, manage, and share it in real time. This requirement is intensified by faster access to information through higher bandwidth capabilities, mobile devices, and disruptive technologies.

Integrating all of this information across silos is a common challenge that hampers access and productivity. The volume of enterprise content is impacted by the departments it must flow through. In many organizations, information is maintained in siloed repositories. Information that should flow securely and effortlessly across departments, partners, suppliers, and customers—on premise and in the cloud—is disconnected and processes are fragmented. As a result, businesses do not have a consolidated view of their information, which means they do not have a consolidated view of their resources, projects, or customers.

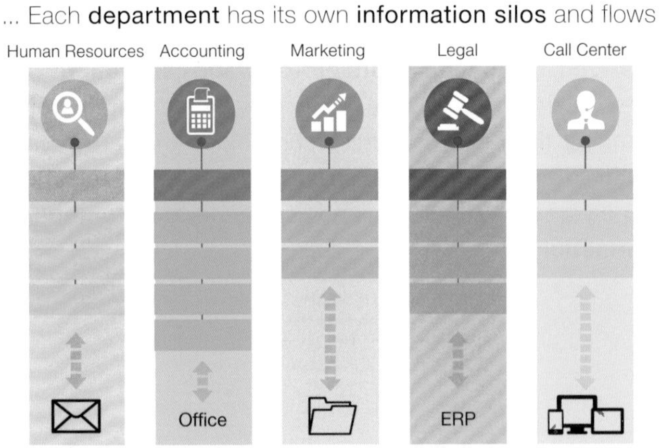

FIGURE 3.4: Integrating Information Across Silos is a Common Challenge

Information chaos reduces margin. Data is expensive due to storage costs and the resources required to manage it. Mismanaged information can cost the enterprise millions of dollars in expenses associated with litigation, regulatory compliance, and e-discovery. Data fragmentation diminishes the value an enterprise can derive from its information flows. Currently, as little as 28 percent of global organizations are gaining strategic value from their content.[11] Most organizations struggle with siloed information and connecting processes across the enterprise. Often, the enterprise must overcome technical, organizational, and cultural hurdles to manage information as an asset.

Big Data = Big Headaches

At present, the volume of enterprise information continues to create big headaches for CIOs and IT leaders—from management to infrastructure, storage, resourcing, and security. Current technologies and architectures are not equipped to handle massive amounts of information. As their "digital footprint" increases, consumers are wary of marketers and governments using their data to serve their own agendas. Security and privacy are important issues associated with information. To cope in 2020, the digital enterprise will need to rethink its data management infrastructure, especially since information will be core to implementing a digitization strategy. Organizations will need to invest in EIM solutions and acquire the skills needed to maximize the value of their information.

The Technology Gap

The right resources have to be in place to analyze information effectively. For many organizations, their data accumulates too quickly, outpacing the ability to use it to their advantage. To meet the demands of growing amounts of data, organization must have processing and storage requirements in place, and the size and scale of these systems makes them costly to manage. Cloud computing offers affordable solutions for storage and analysis on large data sets that could not previously be accessed. While CIOs are focused on minimizing the cost of storage, backups, and security, cloud computing offers affordability, flexibility, and scalability.

In order to benefit from their information, organizations will need to ascertain how much information they can store, how much storage costs, and for how long they need to retain the information. Deploying the technology required to capture, manage, protect, and even dispose of data is a good first step. Data must be discoverable, accessible, and usable for it to have value. It is important to manage this data according to regulations and corporate policies and procedures—ensuring that analysis and release of information is legal and compliant.

---

[11] *"Cisco Connected World Technology Report"*, Cisco, 2012, *http://www.cisco.com/c/en/us/solutions/enterprise/connected-world-technology-report/index.html* (accessed June, 2014).

The Skills Gap

The right people with the right skill set must be put into place to own and manage information initiatives across organizations. Due to its diversity, information will require people with diverse skill sets to manage it. New information-related roles are already emerging and will dictate requirements for a new IT structure to support roles related to information leadership, innovation, and strategy.

There is already a skills gap in expertise required to collect, mine, and analyze big data. The demand is there, and it will reach 4.4 million jobs globally by 2015. The majority of these roles—two thirds—will not be filled.[12] To capitalize on their information, organizations will need to adopt technology enablers and create strategies—as well as applications—around information. Culture will shift to one that engenders open knowledge sharing. Competition will be based on the ability to analyze information for insight and customer information. The better the information, the faster and more precisely an organization can meet consumer needs. The enterprise will need to find a balance between the opportunities provided by information and the risks it presents in privacy and security.

No Risk, No Reward

Despite the potential benefits that access to greater amounts of data brings to society, there are growing concerns around security and privacy. Many large companies are already the gatekeepers of private information and are susceptible to information leaks, which raises the question—how much control do we actually have over our own personal information? How will government and regulators be able to monitor and protect huge amounts of personal data stored in the cloud?

Your digital shadow is the sum of all data left by your interactions in a digital environment. As we rely more on technology, these digital shadows will only grow

FIGURE 3.5: Growing Information Shadows

[12] "Gartner Reveals Top Predictions for IT Organisations and Users for 2013 and Beyond", Gartner, Inc., October 24, 2012.

People are suspicious about the ways that organizations make use of their personal information. As consumers, we move through our days leaving data traces—from time spent on Facebook to purchases we make both off and online, texts sent, video surveillance footage, and the energy consumed in our house. These data traces make up an individual's digital shadow. As we become increasingly reliant on technology, and this technology becomes more interconnected, digital shadows will only grow to become rich, varied, and abundant.

In 2020, businesses will need to find ways to reward consumers in exchange for their data, based on loyalty and trust. Marketers will become more sophisticated in their use of personal data. In his book *Who Owns the Future*, Jaron Lanier posits that individual consumers will sell their personal data to organizations like Google and Facebook that are currently benefiting from collecting vast amounts of it for free. Today, one consumer is taking charge of his personal data and auctioning it off on Kickstarter. The practice of selling off personal data is expected to increase by triple digit percentages by the end of 2014.[13]

In a digital-first world, all individuals will have a commercial identity based on their own personal information. Governments and organizations will have to protect these identities by investing in systems that secure personal information and protect privacy. The number of cyber-attacks on organizations is already impacting spending on information security. Worldwide investment is expected to reach $76.9 billion in 2015.[14]

Alongside security and privacy, intellectual property rights is another legal issue that will need to be closely managed in 2020, especially in light of emerging technologies that facilitate digital printing and production. Questions about property rights and fair use will need to be addressed as data is increasingly duplicated and used in combination with other data. These issues are examined in greater detail in Chapter 7, "Digital Governance".

Where's the Value?

So how does the enterprise find value—and find it quickly—in the mass of unstructured and unmanaged information? The solution to this problem lies partially in its root cause. The network effect, both inside and outside the firewall, has empowered organizations to collect volumes of data at a high velocity across many channels. Based on this data, organizations can determine context. This is where value is created. Organizations can take advantage of location or presence to tailor offerings to match individual preferences or proximity—on either side of the firewall.

---

[13] *"Gartner Top Predictions 2014: Plan for a Disruptive, but Constructive Future"*, Gartner, Inc., October 7, 2013.

[14] Bob Violino, *"Information Security Spending to reach $71 Billion in 2014"*, Information Management, August 25, 2014, http://www.information-management.com/news/information-security-spending-to-reach-71-billion-in-2014-10026010-1.html (accessed August 2014).

Deeper connections allow for instant action to be taken, transactions to occur, and experiences to be created. Technologies such as mobile apps and self-service kiosks are helping organizations tap into the digital lifestyle of both their workforce and consumers. Digital exchanges are immediate; in the future, the digital enterprise will have much tighter connections of each node in a complex series of both internal and external applications. All of this will depend on information and the technology that conveys, stores, and manages it.

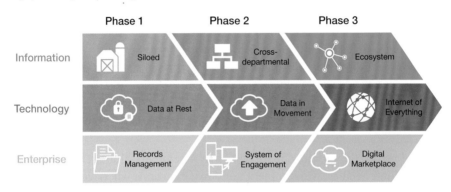

FIGURE 3.6: The Value of the Information Ecosystem

The digital enterprise of the future will be part of an information ecosystem in which data can be shared across the whole value chain, flowing from employeees to partners, suppliers, and customers. Business intelligence, sentiment analysis, social media analytics, content analytics, and predictive analysis will be applied as a complex mix of data to enable the enteprise to act on events and information without human intervention. Information will be consolidated across silos in an organization; the front office will connect seamlessly with the back office. Users will engage with the ecosystem based on their own preferences and data. Organizations like Distell, featured below, are realizing that there is value beyond improved efficiencies and reduced costs in connecting enterprise information and making it more transparent.

Distell

Distell is Africa's leading producer and marketer of spirits, fine wines, ciders, and Ready-To-Drinks (RTDs). It employs nearly 5,000 people and has an annual turnover in excess of 1 billion USD. With 3,000 users of its IT systems spread across 80 office locations worldwide, including specialist teams in remote locations, Distell was struggling to manage growing amounts of decentralized data. Wouter van den Heever, Distell's Enterprise Content Manager, had a vision to digitize this explosion of unstructured information to help improve productivity and empower the Company to differentiate itself and evolve on a global scale. A digital solution was implemented to harness the wealth of intellectual capital in the company and manage information as a corporate asset. What follows are highlights of an interview with Wouter van den Heever describing how he guided this transformation and the benefits the company realized.

FIGURE 3.7: Distell – Achieving Global Differentiation

"As a business with more than 100 brands, there was little opportunity to share best practices between teams. This not only impaired the company's efficiency, but also our ability to collaborate and innovate.

When we implemented our EIM solution, we didn't go for a 'Big Bang' approach across the whole business: we found departments that wanted to digitize their paper-based processes or prove good governance or log ongoing innovations. We focused on these initiatives and brought in a collaborative, searchable, secure repository to enable marketing, sales, operations, production, and service functions in one continent to access information from peers across the globe.

With the system, Distell has doubled the number of users collaborating and sharing information. Today, there are over 13 million information assets in the Distell repository, with tens of thousands of items being added weekly. Distell has doubled the number of users collaborating and sharing information. Ideas are now logged, reviewed, and tracked electronically, where before they were siloed and untraceable. Each business unit has teams incentivized to come up with new ideas, large or small. Previously these ideas might have been written on a whiteboard; now they're in the system. It means a warehouse or production line manager in Johannesburg, for example, can look for ideas used by a similar business unit in Cape Town. Teams are learning from one another.

A big benefit of the EIM system is productivity. Employees can now work anywhere and access their information from any device—from their laptop, tablet, or mobile phone. Another big benefit is employee empowerment based on the ability to share and access useful information, which enables staff to work more effectively for the good of the business. There is a readily available library of corporate documentation for any topic. If someone wants a business plan for the launch of a Two Oceans wine into Canada, it's there. They have it.

The system has helped create a global business with world-class information systems and has fostered a culture of collaboration, ideation, and inclusion. As long as the Internet evolves, so will our digital solution."

Unstructured Information: Today's Untapped Resource

Information is today's untapped resource. When information is managed effectively, it reveals larger patterns of activity to confirm performance levels, evaluate compliance, or deliver customer insight that can differentiate products and services. But how will organizations find, analyze, and act on data to realize its full potential? Being able to capture, preserve, manage, and build information-oriented applications is the next frontier of competitive business. For the last 30 years, CIOs have been focused on automating processes and transactions for structured data with Enterprise Resource Planning (ERP) systems. In the decades to come, CIOs will concentrate on digitizing processes and transactions for unstructured information.

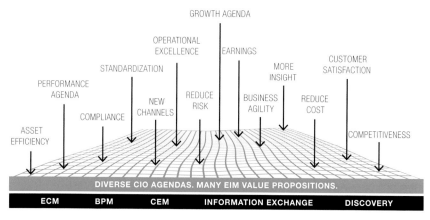

FIGURE 3.8: Creating Business Value With Information

When unstructured enterprise information is well managed, a company's information becomes powerful through the use of information-oriented applications. An enterprise with sound control over information and a robust information architecture can start to deploy or build applications designed to solve the problems of its workforce. The more effectively organizations can collect, find, and process information in the context of an application, the more effectively its employees and operations function.

In 2020, the enterprise will unlock the value of its data through information-based processes for suppliers, employees, customers, financial, cases, projects, and contracts. The list of potential information-based applications is inexhaustible; the only limit is the capacity to gather and manage unstructured information and the requirements of the business.

Currently, only one third of an organization's business processes rely on digital technology.[15] In 2020, *all* of an organization's information and processes will be digital, moving the value of information beyond optimizing performance to create new products and services and open up new sales channels. The forecasted benefits are substantial. An automated mortgage-application process, for example, can reduce costs by up to 70 percent[16]. A digital case management solution results in almost 40 percent improvement in the time it takes to manage cases at a leading financial institution. Retailers can automatically manage in-store inventory for savings in time and more satisfied customers. Governments are turning to self-service case management programs to empower citizens to manage their own information requests and streamline the entire process for public servants. But the most savvy business leaders are realizing that the opportunities to create value move well beyond data warehouses and existing business processes.

Migrating current information-centric processes to digital processes is an overwhelming prospect. The required approach is a break from the past and existing processes to reinvent new processes using digital technologies. The outcome produces myriad benefits, including the ability to increase transparency, monitor performance, mitigate risk, foster innovation and growth, and even create opportunities to monetize data directly.

Increase Transparency

Eighty percent of companies in a recent survey agreed that the pressure for corporate transparency has never been greater.[17] The enterprise is accountable to shareholders, customers, employees, and legislative pressures, as shown in Figure 3.9. Greater transparency into information increases accountability and reduces instances of fraud. Organizations can make use of information to identify anomalies in data, duplicated efforts, errors, and opportunities for cost savings. Data from different sources and departments can be combined to identify productivity gaps. Greater levels of transparency save time and money and help to optimize performance and resources for maximum efficiency.

---

[15] Murray, Sarah, *"CEO Briefing 2014 - The Global Agenda: Competing in a Digital World"*, Accenture, 2014.

[16] Ibid.

[17] Ibid.

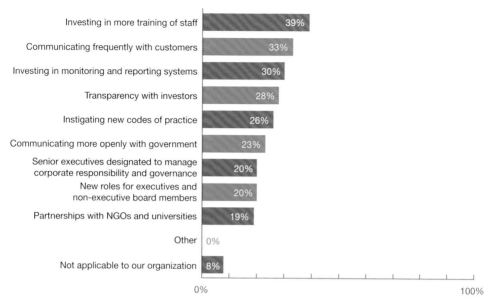

Investing in more training of staff — 39%
Communicating frequently with customers — 33%
Investing in monitoring and reporting systems — 30%
Transparency with investors — 28%
Instigating new codes of practice — 26%
Communicating more openly with government — 23%
Senior executives designated to manage corporate responsibility and governance — 20%
New roles for executives and non-executive board members — 20%
Partnerships with NGOs and universities — 19%
Other — 0%
Not applicable to our organization — 8%

FIGURE 3.9: The Impact of Transparency on the Enterprise[18]

Monitor Performance

Many managers feel they do not have all the information they need to effectively run their departments. Information can be used to support the decision-making process at each step in a business process. Data sets can be combined into management dashboards and comparative engines can be used to measure the effectiveness of projects. Variability in performance can be revealed. Organizations can add value to information by continually measuring impact. As a result, insight can fuel continual performance improvements, learning, and growth across the entire enterprise ecosystem.

Lock-In Security

The need for security has never been more pressing with information fragmented across mobile devices, multiple applications, in both private and public clouds. In all sectors, the ever-present threat of security breaches is driving investments in secure information management. Data consolidation across networks with security mechanisms built right into the system, along with secure information exchange and governance technologies work together to protect information and identify suspicious patterns that require immediate action.

---

[18] Murray, Sarah, "CEO Briefing 2014 - The Global Agenda: Competing in a Digital World", Accenture, 2014.

Augment Compliance and Governance

The requirements for governance and compliance will only increase as governments create more laws and legislation. With information flowing across many channels, the lack of governance policies blocks information's path to value. Aligning processes and information on a common infrastructure protects assets while helping to ensure compliance. Procedural guidance can be more readily combined with documentation, process execution tools, reporting and audits, and ERP systems. An integrated information architecture acts as a central nervous system to capture, track, and report on regulatory requirements. By automating processes and integrating information, organizations can transform risk into opportunity by being able to react to changes in regulations more quickly than their competitors.

Improve Productivity

Making information available and searchable frees up valuable time, so resources can be allocated to focus on top priorities. When information is combined across departmental systems and processes, it is easier to access and duplicated efforts (and data) are reduced—saving time and money. Automated solutions eliminate the need for business users to sort and classify growing amounts content. With a holistic and consolidated information system, information can be analyzed to identify costs savings and opportunities to increase overall productivity.

Optimize Engagement

In 2020, organizations will build apps and services that apply information to create new engagement models for customers, employees, and partners. Inside the enterprise, these new engagement models will create a knowledge-sharing culture that enriches intellectual capital.

FIGURE 3.10: A Digital Workplace

A digitally based "open workplace" connects people with their peers, resources, and information. Digital workplaces are built on EIM tools that disseminate knowledge to all employees. Tools like wikis and blogs are used in a variety of ways to provide employees with a platform for exchanging and managing the information used to accomplish everyday tasks. Project teams can form on the fly and organize themselves around a defined purpose. In one study, innovation rates rose by as much as 20 percent and employees experienced a 35 percent increase in access to expertise—all through accessing a digital workplace.[19]

Increase Customer Insight

Digital technologies like predictive and sentiment analysis help organizations to better understand their consumers and tailor products and services to meet their needs. Analyzing information in new ways surfaces relevant topics, summaries, sentiments, and relationships to deliver more enriched information. Trends and patterns can be revealed by monitoring system information. Insight into customer personas, behavior, and pathways gives organizations the ability to deepen customer engagement, exceed expectations, and create a lifetime of customer value.

Promote Open Data and Economic Opportunity

In a digital-first world, data is the raw material for new products and services. Spear-headed by governments across the globe, the open sharing of information is bringing together software developers, information architects, business leaders, urban planners, scientists, academics, and entrepreneurs to create business value from data.

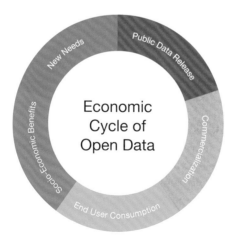

FIGURE 3.11: The Economic Cycle of Open Data

[19] Andrew McAfee, "Enterprise 2.0 is Vital for Business", FT.com, December 9, 2009, http://www.ft.com/cms/s/0/2c473802-e4c4-11de-96a2-00144feab49a.html#axzz375JRalwe (accessed July, 2014).

As of this year, there are one million open datasets made available by governments around the world[20], representing a global trend toward openness that necessitates the sharing of information between governments, their employees, citizens, and private-sector partners. There are many areas where the analysis of large datasets can be of tremendous value. Along with increasing transparency and accountability, the high-level benefits of open data include creating a more participatory government through approaches like crowdsourcing, citizen empowerment, economic development, improved efficiency and productivity, and new meanings based on context and combined sets of data.

Open data is good for the economy. In 2013, geospatial data as the foundation for many map- and weather-based applications was estimated to generate $270 billion in global revenue. Once opened up, information based on water quality, border wait times, health trends, flight tracking, and crime statistics can be accessed and transformed into user-friendly applications to improve the lives of all people. The open movement extends inside the firewall to create an open community model for the enterprise—one that organizes itself around talent, resources, and projects to drive greater productivity and innovation.

Drive Innovation

As we have seen with the open movement, organizations can apply information to ignite innovation, form new partnerships, and drive business outcomes to create competitive advantage. In 2020, consumer input will become critical in product development. The development of new products and services will evolve from sprints to "hyper-connected dashes" in 2020. Product features will be crowdsourced and collective. Feedback about consumer experience with products and services will be collected to upgrade features, improve delivery, and serve niche markets—in real time—removing the developer "safety net". Data-based product ideas will be shared across yottabytes (one trillion terabytes) of data and millions of people as innovation cycles become faster, compressed, and even approach the spontaneous.

Create New Revenue Streams

As information becomes increasingly accepted as a corporate asset, the pressure to measure and maximize its value will increase accordingly. The digital enterprise will discover additional opportunities to monetize information directly, based on packaging data for a price for partners, suppliers, customers, or the market at large. Digital technology is an enabler of the syndication of data. In 2020, individuals as well as organizations will be taking advantage of opportunities to monetize their data and create additional revenue streams.

[20] Douglas Laney and Andrew White, *"Agenda Overview for Information Innovation and Governance"*, 2014, Gartner, Inc., January 10, 2014.

Goods are becoming more digitally sourced. In the future, they will be based on digital designs, plans, and data. The digitalization of products, services, processes and overall business models will demand a disciplined approach to managing, governing, and innovating with information. Effective information management gives organizations the ability to manage information as a tangible asset. As discussed further in Chapter 9, Enterprise Information Management (EIM) is a set of technologies and practices that maximizes the value of information while minimizing its risks.

Linking EIM to Business Value

As the year 2020 approaches, one thing is certain: digital information will be ubiquitous and managing it will be key to success. Currently less than 15 percent of organizations are implementing strategic information management to drive their projects and outcomes. This is changing as more organizations are realizing the strategic importance of managing their information effectively in a digital-first world.[21]

As data is commoditized, organizations will uncover and apply unique information for differentiation. The closer and tighter the connections between structured and unstructured data, the more value can be extracted from it. Bringing this information together—connecting business suites with information suites—is a unifying force that produces a powerful foundation for innovation.

While ERP and other structured data-source platforms have been optimized over the past 30 years, EIM presents rich business opportunity. EIM replaces the disjointed and paper-based system of the past with a consolidated and digitized single source of the truth. EIM technologies support information in its many formats to connect information for deeper insight, better performance, and greater opportunity. We'll take a closer look at how competitive advantage is created through managing consumer-related information in the next chapter, "Digital Engagement".

---

[21] Michele Goetz, *"Are Data Governance Tools Ready for Data Governance?"*, Forrester Research, June 25, 2014, *http://blogs.forrester.com/michele_goetz* (accessed July 2014).

DIGITAL ENGAGEMENT

CHAPTER 4
Digital Engagement

"Digital businesses understand that if they are to win in the age of the customer, customer experience is their only differentiator."[1]

In the "Age of the Customer" focus on the customer is a strategic imperative. As consumers become more connected, they are demanding more from the brands they love. They want access to the information, products, and services they need, when they need them. Location and time are no longer constraints. Communication must be immediate, relevant, and contextual. As the brand experience moves online it must be personalized, intuitive, always on, seamless, and global. Organizations that can deliver engaging brand experiences will dominate their markets now and into the future.

Strategy for Customer Experience

FIGURE 4.1: Digital Experience Is the Key Differentiator[2]

As illustrated above, the digital customer experience is becoming a key differentiator. Business leaders are realizing the importance of a customer-centric approach: in a recent survey, 66 percent of CEOs regard customer relationships to be a key source of sustained economic value and 73 percent are investing heavily in customer insights.[3] This has become even more critical as digital disruption minimizes the barriers to entry in many industries.

---

[1] Nigel Fenwick and Martin Gill, *"The Future of Business Is Digital"*, Forrester Research, March 10, 2014.

[2] Rogowski, Ron, *"The Unified Customer Experience Imperative"*, Forrester Research, May 7, 2013.

[3] Kerry Bodine and Ron Rogowski, *"2013 Customer Experience Predictions"*, Forrester Research, January 3, 2013.

In 2020, delivering digital experiences that exceed expectations will give organizations competitive advantage. As the world becomes more connected and more information is shared, the digital enterprise will be given opportunities to deepen engagement with its customers. The challenge will be to extract value from information, optimize and personalize the delivery of this information, and manage it securely. In a customer-centric era, brands must deliver compelling experiences fueled by a contextual understanding of their customers, while adhering to established information governance policies and standards.

The Empowered, Digital Consumer

Customer experience is defined as the sum of all experiences over the duration of a relationship between a consumer and an organization that delivers products and services. The ideal outcome is a consistent experience that delivers relevant content, products, and services across multiple touchpoints.

Over the years, customer experience has improved: from mass-producing products to meet consumer need in the Age of Manufacturing (1900); to making these goods highly available outside of the town where factories were located in the Age of Distribution (1960); to giving consumers access to the products they need, when and where they want them in the Age of Information (1990), with the help of Internet and e-commerce. In the Age of the Customer, only the organizations that embrace digital disruption will succeed.[4]

FIGURE 4.2: The Digital Experience Ecosystem

[4] David M. Cooperstein, *"Competitive strategy In The age Of The Customer"*, Forrester Research, October 10, 2013.

Customer experience has evolved into digital engagement, literally following the customer online. Disruptive digital technologies have introduced new channels for distribution and consumption. A complex landscape gives customers instant access to data from websites, apps, mobile and wearable devices, sensors in cars and appliances, and social networks. Digital customers are empowered with information at their fingertips—to check a price, read a product review, rate a product or service, or access peers for advice—at any time, from any place.

Today's consumer is smarter, more technically savvy, mobile, and always connected. They're skeptical about traditional marketing tactics like television advertising, magazine ads, billboards, and direct mail. Instead, they're turning to peers for recommendations about products and seeking out more genuine engagement with the brands they like. They're becoming more transparent with their needs, wants, and doubts—and much of this is happening online.

48%
of people say their colleagues and peers are the two most influential sources of information for making software purchase decisions

Base: 2,444 North American and European software decision makers

FIGURE 4.3: Consumers Today Rely on Peer-to-Peer Influence

Empowered consumers are using digital technology to exert their influence and demand quality, price, and service from the world's leading brands. The number of mobile phones is currently over one million globally.[5] If the current pace of adoption is maintained, most of the projected eight billion people on Earth will be online by the year 2025. This is a large and powerful group, and businesses must respond quickly to serve the digital customer in the ways they now dictate.

[5] "Smartphone Users Worldwide Will Total 1.75 Billion in 2014", eMarketer, January 16, 2014, http://www.emarketer.com/Article/Smartphone-Users-Worldwide-Will-Total-175-Billion-2014/1010536 (accessed September 2014).

Social and Mobile Shoppers

Today's consumer has access to a wide variety of technologies. The average American household now supports an Internet-connected computer (80 percent), high-definition TVs (83 percent), and mobile phones (65 percent) with plans to invest in digital recorders, gaming consoles, and smart TVs. U.S. consumers are already subscribing to services like Netflix to stream video—and many are using mobile devices to watch them.[6]

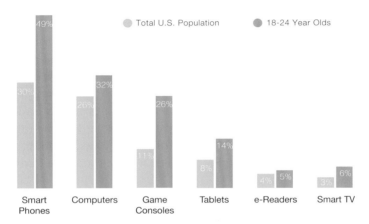

FIGURE 4.4: Planned Technology Investments in U.S. Households[7]

Mobile devices in particular are revolutionizing the digital experience and pushing the limits of engagement. Mobile shoppers represent a shift toward a mobile-centric lifestyle in which information, goods, and services are increasingly accessed through mobile devices. Today, nearly half of mobile consumers rely on mobile devices to research product information and compare prices. In the future, this usage will be surpassed by mobile purchases. According to research, the number of mobile transactions is due to rise 65 percent between now and 2016. In Australia in 2012, mobile retail constituted 30 percent of all digital sales. It is predicted that mobile e-commerce revenues in Europe will rise from $2.17 billion in 2011 to $25 billion by 2017 to constitute 6.8 percent of web sales.[8] Over the next few years, roughly eight out of ten digital shoppers will also be mobile shoppers.

[6] "The Digital Consumer", The Nielsen Company, February 2014.

[7] Ibid.

[8] "7 Ways the Mobile Consumer Changes Everything", Bazaarvoice, 2014.

As consumers continue to take advantage of mobile browsing and shopping, there is a huge opportunity for marketers to support the complete customer journey—from initial interest to purchase and follow-on support. From consumers making price comparisons to making purchases on their handheld devices, rating their experiences, and joining an online community to share reviews, mobile commerce is empowering consumers and providing the enterprise with new ways to engage with their customers.

As mobile retail becomes commonplace, a digital marketplace will evolve to support a range of technologies used to support mobile transactions. Mobile payment and Mobile Financial Services (MFS) will become integral to the functions of financial institutions, banks, and global retailers. Digital banking cards will be embedded in mobile devices and used by 70 percent of physical bank-card users.[9] In addition to card readers, QR codes and Near Field Communications (NFC)—a wireless communications technology that enables mobile devices to communicate based on proximity—will increasingly allow for payment at the point of sales using just a SIM card. In the future, NFC will expand to support other uses, including identification, transportation, and ticketing. Online payment options, such as PayPal® and Square®, will continue to rival traditional payment methods.

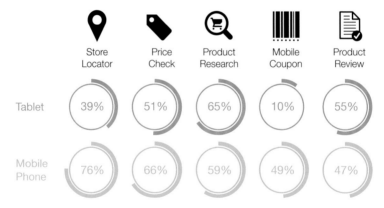

FIGURE 4.5: The Most Popular Activities Among Mobile Shoppers[10]

[9] Garry Evans, "Disruptive Technologies: Winners and losers from game changing innovation", HSBC Global Research, October 2013.

[10] "The Digital Consumer", The Nielsen Company, February 2014.

Like mobility, social media empowers consumers by giving them direct access to their favorite brands in online communities and social networks. Almost two-thirds of social media users visit social media sites at least once a day using a computer, and half of all smartphone users in the U.S. visit social media sites every day.[11] As shown below, social media usage happens in locations that are convenient to consumers.

Social media has found its way into the marketing mix as an effective channel. Websites that contain social media enjoy a 55 percent increase in web traffic.[12] People are more likely to buy (64 percent) from organizations that help them make a purchase using social media channels.[13]

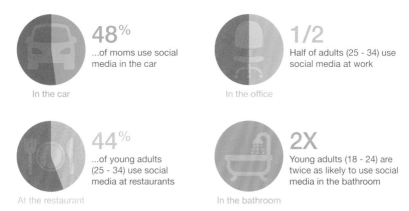

48%
...of moms use social media in the car

In the car

1/2
Half of adults (25 - 34) use social media at work

In the office

44%
...of young adults (25 - 34) use social media at restaurants

At the restaurant

2X
Young adults (18 - 24) are twice as likely to use social media in the bathroom

In the bathroom

FIGURE 4.6: Social Media Usage - Where it Happens[14]

As technology evolves and disrupts, the enterprise will have to adapt and change its communications channels to suit its customers: mobile apps will continue to aid in knowledge sharing, YouTube will replace TV ads, and Twitter® will become a customer support lifeline. But digital consumers are doing more than just online research and retail purchasing—in many cases they are working with organizations and governments to crowdsource new products and services and crowdfund new enterprises. They have entered the supply chain, and by 2020, they will dictate how organizations design, develop, market, sell, and support products and services. They will expect their needs to be met preemptively, through physical and digital touchpoints that may not be familiar places for business interaction, such as a bathroom scale or eyeglasses[15]. And, they will expect access to these touchpoints 24/7.

[11] *"The Digital Consumer"*, The Nielsen Company, February 2014.

[12] Rick Burnes, *"Study Shows Business Blogging Leads to 55% More Website Visitors"*, Hubspot, *http://blog.hubspot.com/blog/tabid/6307/bid/5014/Study-Shows-Business-Blogging-Leads-to-55-More-Website-Visitors.aspx* (accessed 15 Apr. 2013).

[13] *"ComScore"*, invodo, *http://www.invodo.com/resources/statistics/* (accessed March 2013).

[14] *"The Digital Consumer"*, The Nielsen Company, February 2014.

[15] Shar VanBoskirk, *"How to Organize for the Digital Future"*, Forrester Research, March 7, 2013.

A 360-Degree View of the Customer

Like the digital consumer, the digital enterprise that embraces disruptive technologies will also be empowered. As customers increasingly access information, brands, and services online, it's getting easier for the enterprise to follow them based on their interactions. This knowledge, or customer big data, can be used to maximize engagement and create rich, digital experiences.

In 2020, the digital enterprise will rely on analytical tools to paint a holistic picture of the customer, based on information collected at all stages of the customer lifecycle— from purchasing patterns to social networks, website metrics, predictive analytics, and other data mining techniques. Demographic data will be combined with contextual or locational data, channel, sentiment, and behavior to determine customer content preferences and build buyer personas. A deeper understanding of the customer will become a strategic objective. This is a challenge in most organizations today as application silos, departmental silos, and a schism between IT and marketing often prevents organizations from gaining a holistic view of the customer.

Forget the Funnel!

FIGURE 4.7: The Sales Funnel Is Replaced by an Orbital Model

Customer insight will be supported by designated teams, technologies, and budgets. The digital enterprise will look for data-literacy talents and skill sets that can be used to analyze and interpret data with integrated tools in place to support the entire process. Customer big data will be hoarded and protected as an asset as it grows to a key differentiator. Enterprise systems of record will have to merge with systems of engagement. To gain the coveted 360-degree view of the customer, the digital enterprise will need to manage the complete portfolio of its customer information securely in order to maximize its potential and minimize risk.

Marketers will be forced to find unique ways to inject their programs into consumer-constructed ecosystems of value. The traditional sales funnel will be replaced by an orbital model, centered on the customer and defined by interactions and long-term relationships. Conversations will be direct and feedback immediate. Relationships built on trust will enable marketers to reuse data generated by consumers. In many respects, marketing will act like curators of content, rather than creators, repackaging and distributing user-generated content as trusted content across many channels.

In 2020, CMOs will need to drive customer intelligence into sales, services, support, and product development to create meaningful engagement, distinct experiences, and differentiation. While marketers will be challenged by the number of digital channels available for distribution and consumption, there will be more opportunities to deliver immersive, omnipresent, and fulfilling brand experiences. Behind these experiences, lies access to actionable information that helps deliver seamless, multi-channel engagement.

Mastering Digital Engagement

Today, reaching consumers requires a complex, multifaceted approach across many channels. Emerging digital technologies have created new customer touchpoints with increased interaction, information, and opportunities to engage. In 2020, the digital enterprise will focus on creating a compelling brand experience at every touchpoint through omni-channel delivery, responsive design, digitizing the customer journey, and consolidating customer information across the enterprise to increase brand loyalty and profit margins.

The Medium Is the Message: Omni-Channel Delivery

Despite the push to deliver a consistent, dynamic end user experience, companies are still struggling to understand customer interactions across channels and manage execution using multiple technologies. Recent research reveals that $83 billion in marketing is lost each year due to poor customer experience, recognizing leading companies as ones that are engaging customers across all channels.[16]

The majority of businesses today are using at least six channels to engage with their customers. Leading organizations use seven channels and are laser-focused on ensuring the consistency and relevancy of messages they deliver. This approach achieves superior results in return on marketing investments, customer satisfaction, and revenue.[17]

Consumer interaction with brands is already evolving from multi-channel experience to an omni-channel experience. Multi-channel publishing pushes content to users regardless of their device or location. Omni-channel delivery takes this one step further by focusing on consumer need and behavior, pulling together programs to provide consumers with a consistent brand experience across channels, platforms, and devices.

Single-Channel -> Multi-Channel -> Omni-Channel

FIGURE 4.8: Customer as Hub for Many Channels of Engagement

A consistent experience is based on a "single source of the truth" or consistent customer data. It presents a unified style, tone, voice, and visuals. As customers become more mobile, the consistent experience becomes vital. If a customer visits a retail website on a desktop but then changes to a tablet or phone at the time of purchasing, the interface should maintain the same look, functionality, and content to ensure continuity of experience. Customers don't see individual devices or channels: they look for a consistent and familiar brand experience.

[16] Ingram, Katie, *"US$83 Billion Lost Yearly in Marketing Due to Poor Customer Experience"*, CMSWire, May 29, 2013, *http://www.cmswire.com/cms/customer-experience/ibm-us83-billion-lost-yearly-in-marketing-due-to-poor-customer-experience-021084.php* (accessed June 2014).

[17] Minkara, Omer and Aly Pinder, *"Next-Generation Customer Experience Management"*, Aberdeen Group, 2013.

An adaptive and responsive approach helps marketers fuel an ongoing conversation with a shopper, investor, patient, and more. Using responsive design, businesses can manage a single site that caters to all device platforms, sizes, and resolutions. A single video can be dynamically rendered to adjust to the screen size of a mobile device, a website, and a stadium jumbotron. An adaptive design extends the experience with closed captions or plays the audio in a listener's preferred language. Tethered syndication allows each touchpoint to talk to other available touchpoints to optimize experience. Consistently branded content creates a more satisfying end-user experience, and enables the enterprise to chart the customer journey, while aligning with corporate governance policies.

FIGURE 4.9: Consistent Branding Across Channels and Devices

It's All About the Journey

In 2020, the digital enterprise will have to digitize the entire customer journey. Customer journeys document the experience customers have from initial desire through to fulfillment. This includes all points of engagement or the touchpoints that create the overall brand experience.

Customer journeys are based on data collected across various touchpoints, transactions, interactions, social media sites, and devices. Analyzing this data leads to customer insights—and these must be tied back to actions that drive automated, internal processes and the delivery of content and services. This should all happen on the fly, in response to customer requirements to influence their decisions at the moment of need.

The customer journey featured below depicts a consumer interacting with a preferred automobile brand. A prospect might watch a video commercial posted to YouTube and follow it to the manufacturer's website for more information. From that site, after a few clicks and a product download, they might complete a search for a dealer close to their location. After visiting the dealership, they could close the purchase online, receive a personalized thank-you receipt, and connect to a customized customer self-service portal for support or maintenance information. Sensors or devices in the car could communicate issues directly with the service center to ensure immediate support and customer satisfaction. Along the journey, each piece of media consumed becomes more valuable as details are attached to it. The entire experience is orchestrated to maximize engagement, capture preferences, and facilitate a seamless purchasing experience to help incite repeat or follow-on purchases. The value of this information experience can be optimized by the enterprise to increase empowerment, reach, and insight.

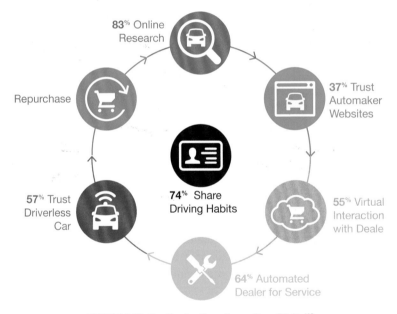

FIGURE 4.10: Car Buying Experience Goes Digital[18]

---

[18] *"Cisco Consumer Experience Report for Automotive Industry: survey of 1,511 consumers in 10 countries"*, Cisco, May 2013.

Currently, only 25 percent of organizations have mapped out their customer journeys for a clear understanding of their experience across multiple touchpoints.[19] Effectively managing customer data is critical to optimizing a customer journey that is more cyclical than it is linear. If an organization can predict customer behavior, it has a better chance at delivering what a customer expects. This is called "contextualization", and it defines digital experiences that adapt to a consumer's context.[20] Content is personalized, anticipating the needs and buying behavior of each consumer to offer location-based products or services at the most opportune moments to buy. To deliver a contextual experience, organizations use tools that combine historical (buying behavior including barcodes or pathways through a website), situational (geo-location), and demographic (profile-based) data. Relevant content is delivered to consumers based on preference, past behavior, and the device they're using, giving organizations opportunities to build brand loyalty and long-term relationships with customers.

Seamless Information Flows

In order to optimize digital engagement, the digital enterprise must understand its customer experience ecosystem, which is a culmination of interactions and transactions between an organization and its employees, partners, suppliers, and customers. A holistic view of the ecosystem helps organizations understand what their customers experience each day and what their employees and partners require in order to support and nurture customers at each stage of their journey.

FIGURE 4.11: Disjointed Digital Engagement

---

[19] Solis, Brian et al., "The 2014 State of Digital Transformation", Altimeter Group, 2014.
[20] Ron Rogowski, "Digital Customer Experience Trends to Watch, 2013", Forrester Research, 2013.

As digital engagement progresses beyond a simple point-and-click, organizations will streamline communications based on integrated information flows across the business. In order to deliver a seamless end-to-end experience across many touchpoints, digital enterprises will need to integrate front- and back-office technologies and processes with a complete information strategy that delivers individualized customer experience at each point of engagement.

Within many organizations, the current technology layers that support customer engagement are multiple and disjointed, consisting of different applications from a variety of vendors. At the customer-facing level, rich digital solutions are required to support the evolution of a brand's publishing points—from tablets and Kindle® devices to Kiosks, gaming consoles, and Google Glass. Behind the customer-facing sites are retail point-of-sale systems (typically tied to inventory) and other applications used by customer-facing employees. Underneath these are the systems ranging from Web Content Management (WCM) to Customer Relationship Management (CRM) systems and various reporting tools. These tools can include web analytics, sentiment analysis, social media monitoring, search engine metrics, business intelligence, sales automation, recommendations engines, and more. In an ideal system, each technology would work to optimize digital engagement and extend to the virtual supply chain. The connections from these systems to customer engagement should be relatively easy to track, but how does the digital enterprise bring this all together for accuracy and consistency?

A unified information management platform empowers employees to effectively create, curate, manage, and monetize information across the create-to-consume process. Using digital technologies to integrate information flows ensures a consistent experience across different contextual interactions, no matter how customers entered the conversation. In the digital enterprise, this holistic approach requires that cross-functional teams work together to deliver a unified experience across multiple touchpoints.

FIGURE 4.12: A Seamless Process - From Create to Consume

Customer Centricity Starts Inside the Firewall

Creating a consistent user experience starts inside the firewall. Teams and departments need to be aligned around customer segments. The strategic CIO has an opportunity to harmonize technology applications with digital engagement across every department in the enterprise. IT departments are already embracing the vast benefits of a well-architected Enterprise Information Management (EIM) platform to create compelling experiences. Engaged employees are more satisfied, productive, and supportive of corporate objectives. Companies that engage all parts of their organization—from back-office staff to frontline employees—are more likely to deliver compelling brand experiences than companies that take a piecemeal approach.

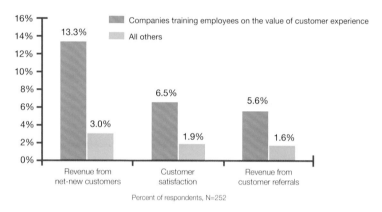

FIGURE 4.13: Linking Customer Experience to Employee Objectives[21]

In the digital enterprise, every employee must understand the influence they have on the customer lifecycle. Organizations that tie customer experience initiatives to employee objectives have seen up to a 10 percent increase in customer satisfaction and customer revenue. As one Auto Company in the U.S. stated: "One of the building blocks of our Customer Experience Management (CEM) activities involves creating engaged employees to improve our customer interaction results and even support new product development efforts."[22]

In the following feature, Citibank exemplifies how the enterprise of today must shift its business models to focus on the customer first as a key differentiator in a crowded marketplace.

[21] Barrenechea, Mark J. and Tom Jenkins, "Enterprise Information Management", OpenText, 2013.

[22] Aberdeen Group, "Customer Experience Management: Using the Power of Analytics to Optimize Customer Delight", Research Preview, Aberdeen Group, http://www.brandchannel.com/images/papers/531_aberdeen_group_wp_customer_experience_management_0911.pdf (accessed February 2013).

Citibank

Citibank is the consumer division of Citigroup, a publically-traded financial services multi-national headquartered in New York City and the largest bank in the U.S. based on total assets. Citibank operates around the world with 3,777 branch locations in 36 countries. In addition to offering standard banking transactions, Citibank markets insurance, credit cards, and investment products. Citibank's online services division is among the most successful in the industry claiming about 15 million users. This success is due in large part to the company's focus on digital innovation. The bank collaborates with technology vendors on leading-edge solutions for their business. Citibank leads the way in terms of adopting new technologies and transforming their services to surpass the expectations of their digital customers.

What follows are excerpts from an interview with Simon Chiang, Head of International Cards, Global Consumer Technology at Citibank. In the interview, Mr. Chiang discusses the bank's state-of-the-art card technology and how the industry has been disrupted by digital technologies and the demands of the digital customer.

FIGURE 4.14: Citibank Introduces New Ways to Pay - Digitally

"The financial services industry has completely transformed itself and its services for the digital customer. As customers become more connected, they want to access their financial information and services online, using their mobile devices, on demand, from any location. They are looking for more convenient and faster ways to make purchases. This has required us to re-invent our processes, moving them online and leveraging technology for fast, accurate, and secure information exchange between consumers, merchants, their banks, and other trading partners.

To support the digital customer, payment methods have evolved. From credit cards, to debit cards, to pre-paid mobile cards, technology enables these digital transactions. In addition, mobile payments—or making payments with a smartphone—are gaining traction with many consumers. The Apple iPhone® 6 and Apple Pay®, for example, provide consumers and merchants respectively with Near Field Communications (NFC) capabilities to enable 'pay-by-touch' transactions. NFC makes use of short-range wireless technologies to detect the customer within short physical distances.

With many exciting technology changes impacting financial transactions, Citibank is launching Apple Pay in the U.S. and it will soon be rolled out to the international market. While mobile payment is gaining traction, broad user acceptance will take some time. People—especially those over the age of 45—are used to carrying and paying with plastic credit cards. They need to be convinced that mobile payment is a secure method of transacting. Despite this barrier to adoption, we predict that within ten years, 50 percent of payment transactions will be made using smartphones. We expect to roll out new merchant terminals with NFC capabilities over the next five to ten years. To support this move to mobile, we are working hard to promote the advantages of mobile payments and drive user acceptance.

We realize security concerns are top of mind for users, especially when they are making payments online or sharing financial information. But a new technology called tokenization introduces heightened levels of security for payments made at point-of-sales (POS) terminals, either by card or by mobile. With tokenization, sensitive customer data is encrypted at the point where it is captured (the card is swiped or detected wirelessly) and sent to the merchant's payment processor where it is decrypted and the transaction is authorized. A token representing the entire transaction is then sent back to the retailer indicating approval. With tokenization, sensitive customer data doesn't reside on the user's device. As well, customer data is not actually shared with the merchant. Instead, it is the token that stays on file and is stored on the merchant's network as proof of purchase.

At Citibank, we are focused on meeting the needs of the digital customer: we stay on the cusp of new advances in technology and we are always exploring innovative ways to serve them. But, ultimately, the technologies we adopt need to improve our customer experience. As our processes move toward digital channels, the customer experience is paramount. We strive to give each customer a consistent experience across all our channels, including their mobile devices, the Internet, ATM, branch, and Interactive Voice Response (IVR) channels. We want our brand to be consistent, regardless of channel, and the experience to be personalized and relevant. Collecting, managing and leveraging customer information allows us to better understand our customers and tailor the Citibank experience to their needs.

To this end, we have invested a lot of resources into the area of predictive analytics. We are using all the consumer data we capture to understand our customer's spending patterns. This data allows us to profile a customer, segment them, and push product or service offerings to him or her at the right time. To do this, we also use geo-fencing to define geographical boundaries around a given retailer—whether it be a store in a mall or a specific POS terminal. When a customer with a relevant profile crosses the boundary, this triggers the delivery of 'location specific' advertisements to their mobile device. Geo-fencing fosters engagement with customers using the most highly contextual, personal, and relevant channel possible: their mobile devices. It's the most targeted advertising a brand can do right now. It's where hyper-local meets hyper-relevant.

Along with helping to deliver an optimized customer experience, mobile and other disruptive digital technologies are significantly impacting the financial services industry. Our business has been transformed and continues to be transformed by new technologies which have changed our markets, shifted our channels, and modified the way we engage and operate. Information and its effective management has given us a competitive edge and helped us not only to succeed but also to establish ourselves as innovators in our industry."

Marketing and IT: Better Together

Successful brands connect employee and channel engagement with the appropriate customer experience. To make this happen, IT departments need to collaborate closely with marketing to deliver satisfying digital experiences—all focused around optimizing customer engagement.

Digital technology has become a key enabler in the delivery of more relevant and richer brand experiences. The marketing toolbox has grown to incorporate new devices, channels, and media into its programs. The CMO of the future will embrace the cloud and social networks to follow customers, listen to what they're saying, engage in conversations with them, build brand, and refine the experience with digital technology. CIOs are responsible for providing consistent customer support using innovative technologies like rich Internet applications, rich media, collaboration tools, social media, and information management.

There is a mutual dependency between IT and marketing in optimizing digital engagement. Marketing is dependent upon IT to implement and maintain the systems of record that marketing uses to run its programs. Emerging systems of engagement, such as NFC-enabled mobile payments at the point of sale, run on systems of record. Marketing needs IT to make sure that these systems function quickly, seamlessly, and securely to build positive brand experiences.

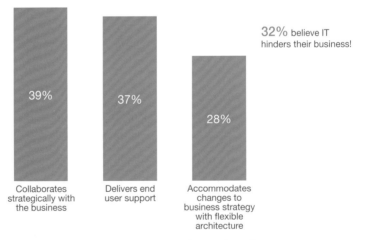

FIGURE 4.15: Marketing and IT - A Mutual Dependency[23]

[23] George F. Colony and Peter Burris, "Technology Management in the Age of the Customer", Forrester Research, October 2013.

The CMO pursues engagement to influence customer satisfaction, brand value, and revenue opportunities. The CIO may be looking to reduce the operational cost of creating, managing, and securing the latest app or supporting multiple mobile devices across the organization. This struggle between the line-of-business and IT is exacerbated by consumer influence. Evolving this relationship into a more collaborative one will require a cultural shift as 32 percent of marketers currently believe that their IT department hinders their own business success.

The digital enterprise can only function as a customer-centric organization if IT and marketing teams work together. This involves tighter mutual dependencies and aligned strategic business objectives focused on the customer. In the future, "tiger teams" made up of cross-functional, task-based teams will focus on applying innovative technologies to engage with end users. Marketers will have dedicated IT resources and IT staff will be marketing-savvy. More time and resources will be dedicated to the creation, management, and measurement of information to help marketers develop and measure the effectiveness of their programs—something that 70 percent of marketers have trouble doing today.

For both IT and marketing departments, embracing an authentic customer-centric strategy requires creating rich and interactive digital experiences that comply with information governance requirements. This necessitates a platform of integrated customer experience capabilities that can be architected to work seamlessly together.

Experience Management Drives Differentiation

As part of a comprehensive EIM strategy, a Customer Experience Management (CEM) solution helps CIOs and CMOs turn unstructured data sources into levers of competitive advantage and profitability. While there are multiple definitions for CEM, they all converge on a similar idea: exceeding customer expectations to improve business results.

A CEM platform combines software applications that help organizations create richer, more interactive digital engagement across devices and channels without sacrificing information governance and compliance. CEM empowers the digital enterprise to capture audience expectations, process requests, search for relevant content, curate user-generated content, assess consumer activities for analysis after the fact, and present actionable data to create exceptional digital experiences. Video, rich media, and personalized content can be created collaboratively, published seamlessly, and shared ubiquitously to surprise and delight customers at every turn.

FIGURE 4.16: CEM Creates Value Across the Customer Lifecycle

In 2020, the digital enterprise will consolidate its customer experience solutions on a single engagement platform. This will empower the enterprise to maximize the potential of its information to reach new markets and gain competitive advantage. As digital disruption triggers the creation of new engagement models, their reach will extend outside the enterprise and all along the supply chain. In the following chapter, we'll take a look at how the digital customer and disruptive technologies are affecting the supply chain and how the digital enterprise can respond with a complete overhaul of its supply chain processes.

DIGITAL SUPPLY CHAIN

CHAPTER 5

Digital Supply Chain

"In 2020 we can expect to see a vibrant and increasingly collaborative environment in which buyers, suppliers, and technology will morph into a just-in-time, market-driven world requiring the right information, in the right form, in the right language, at the right time."[1]

Digital technology is giving rise to global, highly-interconnected, and complex supply chains. In 2020, the digital enterprise will integrate its operations and collaborate seamlessly with partners and suppliers to maintain supply chain excellence while satisfying the expectations of the digital customer. The previous chapter examined how technology-based transformation is impacting the customer experience and engaging customers in new ways. In this chapter, we'll take a look at how digital technology is transforming the supply chain, especially in terms of digital experience, process efficiencies, business integration, data and information, and new products and services.

The "Age of the Customer" will have far-reaching ramifications across the enterprise—from how products are manufactured to how they are marketed, packaged, distributed, and serviced. The enterprise has already stepped up for this challenge by making double-digit increases in digital marketing investment.[2] As organizations micro-segment their markets to deliver tailored products and services, the supply chain must keep pace with rapid-fire cycle of go-to-market activities by supporting integrated and digital processes across the supply chain.

Technology-based transformation is providing core business processes with the flexibility and agility required to compete in a digital-first world. It is also enabling business integration capabilities to keep pace with growing volumes of cross-border exchanges of goods, communications, and commerce.

A Digital Ecosystem of Suppliers

In 2020, an organization as a standalone entity with a linear value chain will be replaced by the digital enterprise, operating within a dynamic network of suppliers and partners. From within this extended enterprise ecosystem, businesses can assemble new or complimentary capabilities from other suppliers and more easily pivot their operations to meet demand.

---

[1] Mike Lacobucci, *"Looking ahead to globalization 2020"* MultiLingual Computing,
  http://www.moravia.com/files/download/Globalization2020_MultilingualComputing.pdf (accessed July 2014).

[2] Michael Burkett, Steven Steutermann, Noha Tohamy, *"Digital Marketing, Internet of Things and 3D Printing are Digital-Business-Driven Disruptions for Supply Chains"*, Gartner, Inc., March 11, 2014.

Distributed manufacturing is a good example of a dynamic and flexible supply chain model. In distributed manufacturing, the Original Equipment Manufacturer (OEM) contracts out manufacturing to partner factories located close to consumers to reduce costs, environmental impact, and delivery times and to deliver customized products to a local market.[3] Manufacturing operations can be added, scaled, or eliminated based on the orders received and the markets targeted.

As supply chains morph into dynamic systems, the digital supply chain will rely on third parties for contract manufacturing, logistics management, warehousing, and transportation. Digital technology is making this integrated model possible by enabling specialized companies to communicate, collaborate, and exchange real-time information. The end result is a tightly interconnected network of business partners collaborating to serve the digital customer. By embracing emerging technologies, the digital supply chain can deliver the improved efficiencies and performance required to better manage change, complexity, and globalization.

A Global, Digital-First Economy

A global economy is putting strains on today's supply chain as it struggles to assimilate increasing amounts of goods, commerce, and communications exchanged across borders. Digital technology makes it possible for a small company or even an individual to participate in the global economy—from anywhere in the world. Lower barriers to entry result in higher levels of competition from all parts of the globe, enabling emerging economies to play a much larger role in the global economy.

Based on stiffer competition, businesses are focusing on their area of specialty and outsourcing other operations. They are migrating from a vertically integrated model in which end-to-end supply chain activities are managed in-house to a highly-specialized, highly-outsourced supply chain model. In the computer industry, for example, OEMs are retaining operations within their area of specialty and outsourcing component manufacturing to contractors who buy the parts, assemble the devices, and perform quality control.

While this model is prevalent in manufacturing, organizations in every business sector are outsourcing everything from customer service, tax, accounting, and IT to strategic planning, public relations and marketing. In fact, it's difficult to name an industry that has not become highly specialized and dependent on business partners for success.[4]

---

[3] Adam Robinson, *"The Rise of Distributed Manufacturing and 7 Advantages over Traditional Manufacturing"*, Cerasis blog, April 2, 2014, *http://cerasis.com/2014/04/02/distributed-manufacturing/* (accessed July 2014).

[4] Steve Keifer, *"Herding Geese: The Story of the Information Supply Chain"*, 2011.

With an increased number of businesses participating in the global economy, prosperity around the world is rising, especially in emerging economies. As illustrated in Figure 5.1, while it took 154 years for the U.K. to double their per capita Gross Domestic Product (GDP) during the Industrial Revolution, China and India have doubled their per capita incomes in one-tenth of that time.[5] As a result, the new economy is expected to herald in an additional 1.8 billion consumers in 2025, nearly all from emerging markets.[6] As these populations pursue economic interests, global consumption and cross-order trade will explode, further impacting the supply chain.

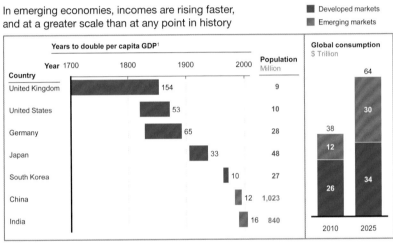

1 Time to increase per capita GDP in purchasing power parity (PPP) terms from $1,300 to $2,600.

FIGURE 5.1: Rapid Rise in Emerging Economies' Incomes[7]

Exploding Cross-Border Trade

Over the last few decades, there has been an enormous explosion in cross-border trade, and these volumes will grow further. Between 1980 (1.8 trillion) and 2011 (17.2 trillion), there was a tenfold increase in cross-border trade with volumes poised to increase by 2025 (64 trillion). Nearly 60 percent of this increase will take place between emerging economies[8]. The challenge for supply chains will be to support growing volumes of cross-border transactions while maintaining performance, security, and compliance with both local and international regulations.

[5] "Global Flows in a Digital Age: How Trade, Finance, People, and Data Connect the World Economy", McKinsey & Company, April 2014.

[6] Ibid.

[7] Ibid.

[8] Ibid.

As cross-border trade grows, the nature of the goods will change. Physical goods will be digitized into virtual goods and services. These transactions will trigger greater volumes of knowledge-based exchanges—goods and activities that have a high Research and Development (R&D) component, require highly skilled labor, and involve the exchange of information, ideas, and expertise.

Underlying all this cross-border trade and commerce are exchanges of data and communications. There has been a sevenfold increase in data and communication flow between regions and occurring across emerging economies from 2008 through to 2013. The chart below illustrates that every major route has increased dramatically and that all routes have become more interconnected.

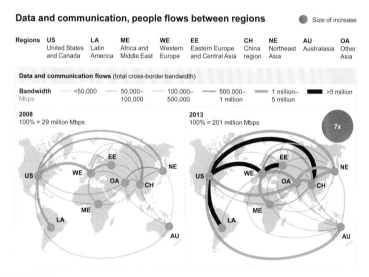

FIGURE 5.2: Sevenfold Increase in Cross-Border Data, Communication, and People[9]

Global transactions have been part of our world for centuries, binding people and economies together across borders. Today, however, the volume of these transactions is rapidly expanding and the pace of exchange is accelerating. In a digital-first world, supply chains will be global, fragmented, dynamic, and complex. They will need to facilitate huge increases in cross-border exchange of physical goods and deal with soaring volumes of cross-border data, communications, and commerce between networks of suppliers. Delivering superior Supply Chain Management (SCM) and responsiveness will depend on tight synchronization of supply and demand data as well as the movement of goods, information, and funds between a large number of logistic and trading partners. Only by leveraging digital technologies will companies achieve the levels of speed, accuracy, and agility required for operational excellence in 2020.

[9] *"Global Flows in a Digital Age: How Trade, Finance, People, and Data Connect the World Economy"*, McKinsey & Company, April 2014.

Accelerating Processes to Hyper-Drive

To meet the challenges of a digital economy, organizations must digitize their business processes. This goes beyond merely converting paper records to electronic or automating process steps. It requires close examination of key corporate processes, understanding the needs of all stakeholders, determining new outcomes based on these needs, then working back and leveraging digital technology to fundamentally reinvent processes.

Ideally, companies should digitize core business processes from end to end, in their entirety. When companies digitize portions of a process, they may achieve improved outcomes but fail to produce an overall seamless experience. A team comprised of external stakeholders and representatives is essential to ensure changes are fully evaluated and cohesive and to take further action to redefine operating models, organizational structures, and roles.

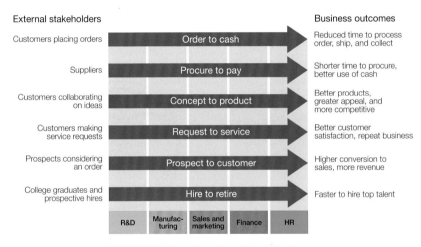

FIGURE 5.3: Cross-Functional Processes[10]

In a digital-first world, each process is critical to empowering the digital enterprise to operate in hyper-drive. The order-to-cash and request-to-service processes are important for rapid fulfillment of products and services. A tightly-interconnected supply chain synchronizes trading partners and shortens the procure-to-pay cycle. Customer insights and cross-functional collaboration fuel the concept-to-product process for fast turnaround of new products and features. In the digital enterprise, technology enables each of these processes to operate seamlessly, efficiently, and rapidly to meet the heightened expectations of customers and drive competitive advantage.

---

[10] Connie Moore, *"The Process-Driven Business of 2020"*, Forrester Research, April 16, 2012.

The benefits of digitizing information-intensive processes are numerous. Costs can be reduced by up to 90 percent and turnaround times improved by several orders of magnitude.[11] Errors can be reduced. New channels and new routes to the customer can be leveraged. Replacing manual paper-based processes with digitized processes and documents allows businesses to collect data to better understand process performance, costs, and risk factors. Real-time reports and dashboards can alert managers to address problems before they become critical. Over and above these benefits, digital technology helps to build more nimble and flexible processes.

Increasing Business Agility

While Logistics is often viewed as a supporting function and a "cost of doing business", a growing number of organizations appreciate its strategic importance. In order to compete, organizations need to maintain superior levels of process excellence, while rapidly responding to the changing needs of their market. Process changes that take months to implement are no longer acceptable or viable. For the digital enterprise, creating processes that are agile and flexible is a strategic priority. This can be accomplished using technologies such as Smart Process Applications (SPAs) and Dynamic Case Management (DCM).

Smart Process Applications

Digital enterprises are leveraging technologies like SPAs to quickly create and adapt processes to the changing needs and expectations of their market. SPAs are an evolution of Business Process Management (BPM) software that uses a "process factory" approach for rapidly deploying new and/or updated case management processes. With SPAs, users can assemble pre-built, ready-to-use software components to create and deploy new service processes in as little as 30 days. Existing processes can be modified just as easily.

Self-service capabilities can be integrated into SPAs to meet consumer expectations for 24/7 engagement. Self-service software allows subject matter experts to automate answers and deliver step-by-step instructions for resolving common customer inquiries. These automated, on-demand decision support systems can engage the customer—anytime, anywhere—and provide instant answers to their questions or inquiries.

---

[11] Shahar Markovitch and Paul Willmott, *"Accelerating the Digitalization of Business Processes"*, McKinsey & Company, May 2014.

Dynamic Case Management

DCM is another emerging technology that brings flexibility to the digital supply chain for *ad hoc* service processes. Traditional BPM solutions automate structured, repeatable processes with minimal human intervention and decision-making, except when exceptions arise. In contrast, DCM solutions are designed to manage processes that are unstructured or *ad hoc* in nature—processes that are not repeatable and often require extensive interaction between human participants to achieve an outcome.[12] These unstructured processes are foundational to the supply chain in service-based and/or knowledge-driven organizations.

FIGURE 5.4: Mobile Case Management

DCM solutions enable an expert to access, review, and process information about a case—deciding the best course of action to achieve a desired outcome. They also bring collaboration to the supply chain by enabling multiple people to share and work together on a given output. Cases can be managed using mobile devices, so case workers can update information while they are located on-site visiting clients.

The speed and agility of supply chain operations will continue to be enhanced by applications that synchronize data and exchange supply chain transactions with increased speed, flexibility, accuracy, and security. In 2020, the digital supply chain will gain many capabilities and advantages offered by B2B e-commerce and operations as they move to the cloud.

---

[12] Diana Davis, *"Case closed? The Difference Between Dynamic Case management (DCM) and Business Process Management (BPM)"*, Process Intelligence Network (PEX), *http://www.processexcellencenetwork.com/business-process-management-bpm/articles/case-closed-the-difference-between-dynamic-case-ma/* (accessed July 2014).

The Information Supply Chain

To effectively orchestrate today's outsourced and distributed supply chain, organizations must tightly coordinate the flow of goods, communications, and commerce across business partners. B2B e-commerce (also called B2B integration) is comprised of a "set of technologies that facilitate the real-time transfer of information, money, goods, and services".[13] Like consumers, businesses need to purchase merchandise, trade stock, and pay bills. B2B e-commerce is the information supply chain that orchestrates transactions for the digital enterprise. With the complexity and frequency of business transactions, B2B e-commerce involves a heightened degree of coordination, data synchronization, and transaction automation.

B2B e-commerce dates back to the 1960s with the use of Electronic Data Interchange (EDI), a standard for exchanging data between companies. Today, however, B2B integration applies to a broader category of technologies that are not only used to purchase goods and services, but also to manage entire supply chains and automate the transactions between various trading partners.

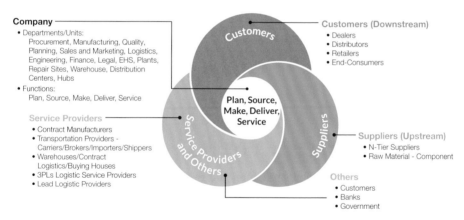

FIGURE 5.5: End-to-End Supply Chain Business Partners[14]

With modern B2B integration platforms, an OEM can automate many of the interactions and transactions in their supply chain—among designers, contract manufacturers, Third-Party Logistic providers (3PLs), distributors, and aftermarket service providers. Automating the order of parts using an electronic catalogue and purchasing exchanges allows for Just-in-Time (JIT) manufacturing, as illustrated in the figure below. Once they are purchased and received, parts, sub-assemblies, and final products can be automatically tracked across the supply chain using sensors or Radio Frequency Identification (RFID) tags, discussed in more detail later on in this chapter.

[13] Steve Keifer, "Herding Geese: The Story of the Information Supply Chain", 2011.

[14] Christian Titze, William McNeill, and Ray Barger Jr, "Multiple Processes, Partners and Data Objects Must be Considered to Obtain Benefits from Supply Chain Visibility", Gartner, Inc., July 25, 2013.

Automating processes is critical for supply chain efficiency and effectiveness. Leading supply chain management organizations, for example, are more likely to incorporate automation tools to synchronize and manage product information and financial flows across the extended global supply chain.[15] B2B integration provides the complete network of supply chain partners with a collaborative, secure, and automated platform for dynamically managing business transactions and delivering the "perfect order"—the right product delivered in full, on time, every time.

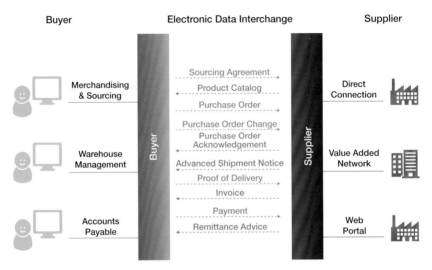

FIGURE 5.6: Automated EDI Transactions Supporting a Retail Purchase

End-to-End Supply Chain Visibility

As today's supply chains become increasingly multifaceted and outsourced, end-to-end supply chain visibility is becoming an important technology for agility and real-time decision-making. Supply chain visibility provides transparency into and management of information that travels across the supply chain and is related to product orders and shipments, including transport and logistics activities and events that occur in transit.[16]

Visibility is gained by tracking objects along the supply chain using sensors, RFID tags, and communicating with enterprise business platforms via EDI. It is also gained by incorporating supply chain status information from any number of other tracking technologies and systems. Supply chain visibility requires the processing of both structured and unstructured information from across the network of suppliers and partners. Once the data is captured, it is sorted and filtered to isolate useful information.

[15] Bob Heaney, "Supply Chain Visibility. A Critical Strategy to Optimize Cost and Service", Aberdeen Group, May 2013.
[16] Ibid.

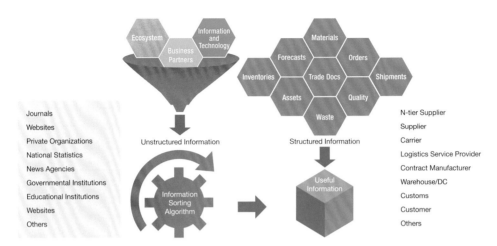

FIGURE 5.7: Structured and Unstructured Data Sources for Improved Visibility[17]

The ultimate goal of supply chain visibility is to enable organizations to respond in a timely manner with real-time decision-making and trade-offs for timely order fulfillment, increased profitability, and reduced risk. If a parts shortage in manufacturing is identified, for example, parts can be replenished but existing supply can also be allocated, and/or customer demand steered away from products containing that part—all according to an automated process.

In response to the pressures brought on by globalization and supply chain intricacy, end-to-end supply chain visibility is becoming a top priority. In a recent study, 85 percent of companies indicated they plan to increase their current level of visibility.[18] As expected, when asked about key pressures driving them to improve visibility (as shown in Figure 5.8), executives identified dealing with the complicated nature of global operations (45 percent) and the need to improve speed and accuracy (43 percent) as top drivers.

Effective strategies for dealing with these pressures include improving visibility into internal supply chain transactions and costs, as well as increasing visibility into external supplier-side processes with partners.[19]

---

[17] Christian Titze, Ray Barger Jr., *"How to Enable End-to-End Supply Chain Visibility"*, Gartner, Inc., January 23, 2014. *http://www.gxsblogs.com/morleym/2013/10/how-the-internet-of-things-will-impact-b2b-and-global-supply-chains.html* (accessed August, 2014)

[18] Bob Heaney, *"Supply Chain Visibility. A Critical Strategy to Optimize Cost and Service"*, Aberdeen Group, May 2013.

[19] Ibid.

FIGURE 5.8: Top Drivers for Supply Chain Visibility[20]

Collaboration in the Cloud

Collaboration across the supply chain requires trading partners to synchronize their master data, gain visibility into the supply chain operations of other partners, and coordinate their efforts to fulfill orders. While these activities have historically occurred via B2B integration on private EDI networks, many companies are now shifting their operations to the cloud.

Achieving this scenario involves a major change in enterprise architecture. As depicted in Figure 5.9, a cloud-based collaboration platform involves the implementation of shared application logic and master data in order to synchronize data and connect processes with each member's internal systems.[21]

Cloud-based platforms for B2B integration are ideally suited to facilitate collaboration between multiple trading partners. With a cloud-based model, each partner across the value chain can place relevant, internal data outside their firewall where it can be exposed for external parties to consume. Collaboration in the cloud ensures all business partners have access to a common source of master data. They can be confident it is accurate and secure.

There are many benefits provided by cloud deployment and, as a result, we are seeing a decided shift to the cloud. Today, although less than 20 percent of the logistics and transportation industry have adopted a Software-as-a-Service (SaaS) model, these solutions are forecasted to increase through 2016 with a 21.4 percent five-year compound annual growth rate.[22] In 2020, increasing numbers of global supply chains will rely on a cloud computing platform for B2B integration and supply chain collaboration.

---

[20] Bob Heaney, *"Supply Chain Visibility. A Critical Strategy to Optimize Cost and Service"*, Aberdeen Group, May 2013.

[21] Christian Titze, William McNeill, Ray Barger Jr, *"Multiple Processes, Partners and Data Objects Must be Considered to Obtain Benefits from Supply Chain Visibility"*, Gartner, Inc., July 25, 2013.

[22] Ibid.

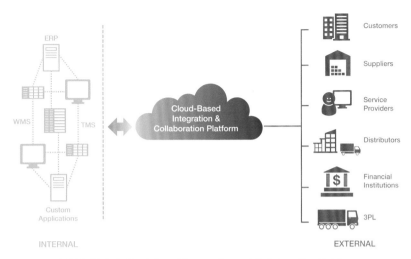

FIGURE 5.9: A Cloud-Based Integration and Collaboration Platform

A Rich Network of Data

The digital supply chain of the future will seamlessly integrate data from across the extended enterprise, and it will include data from the Internet of Things (IoT). While in its infancy today, there will be a thirtyfold increase in web-enabled physical devices by the year 2020 and an IoT that reaches 26 billion installed units.[23]

Data will flow online from wearable technologies like Google Glass, 3-D printers, and logistics drones. All sorts of products, appliances, and equipment will communicate status updates and information. How is this useful to the supply chain? Once the data is captured by a remote device, it is then transferred by fixed wire or wireless communication over the Internet to a B2B integration platform. From here it can be consumed by other devices in the network, including back-office enterprise platforms like Enterprise Resource Planning (ERP) or Enterprise Information Management (EIM).[24]

The presence of these IoT devices will create a network rich with information and insights. This information delivers three primary benefits to the supply chain:[25]

Pervasive Visibility – Information about the physical location of products and/or shipments (from the point of manufacture through to the point of delivery) enables companies to plan operations with greater efficiency, reduce the number of items lost in transit, and fulfill orders with greater accuracy.

---

[23] Michael Burkett, Steven Steutermann, Noha Tohamy, *"Digital Marketing, Internet of Things and 3D Printing are Digital-Business-Driven Disruptions for Supply Chains"*, Gartner, Inc., March 11, 2014.

[24] Ibid.

[25] Mark Morley, *"How the 'Internet of Things' will Impact B2B and Global Supply Chains"*, Driving B2B Blog, Posted October 15, 2013. *http://www.gxsblogs.com/morleym/2013/10/how-the-internet-of-things-will-impact-b2b-and-global-supply-chains. html* (accessed August, 2014).

Proactive Replenishment – Information about the physical location of products and/or shipments enables companies to replenish product as shortages are detected. When applied to retail outlets, sensors in the store shelves, for example, can detect when stock is low and trigger reordering.

Predictive Maintenance – Information about the status of equipment can also be used to order replacement parts and schedule service before the part fails.

Supply Chain Orchestration

As digital technology evolves, more and more businesses will pursue supply chain orchestration. This involves outsourcing end-to-end supply chain activities to a single entity for intensified levels of automation and synchronization.

The shift from collaboration to orchestration occurs in various phases. Historically, supply chain processes have been performed by core business applications executed within a corporate function or silo. These include applications such as Transportation Management Systems (TMS), Warehouse Management Systems (WMS), Supplier Relationship Management (SRM) systems, and other Business Intelligence (BI) applications. These applications provide enterprise visibility into specific functional processes for production and logistics.

The first phase of transformation involves an "integration" phase in which ERP is deployed for additional functionality, to connect data within the silos, and to allow multi-directional communication and interaction within the enterprise.

Next, to enable multi-enterprise collaboration across the supply chain, tools such as a collaboration hub or control tower technology for logistics allow every partner across the supply chain access to a "single source of the truth". Collaboration occurs when all partners in the supply chain work together to make production possible.[26] A cloud-based collaboration platform allows all suppliers and partners to synchronize master data outside their firewall and work together to achieve efficient production and logistics at various locations.

Orchestration occurs above and beyond collaboration, when a single company takes responsibility for operating the entire end-to-end supply chain and provides tight tracking, synchronization, and the secure exchange of goods, communications, and commerce. As described in the story below, Michelin has turned to B2B managed services for orchestrating their global supply chain.

---

[26] N. Viswanadham, *"Orchestration: The New Form of Collaboration"*, InsightOn.

Michelin

Michelin is the world's largest tire manufacturer, notable both for its tire brands (including Michelin, BFGoodrich, Kleber, Tigar, Riken, Kormoran and Uniroyal) and its company mascot Bibendum —colloquially known as the 'Michelin Man'. While the company's global headquarters are located in Clermont-Ferrand in the Auvergne region of France, tire production spans the globe occurring in France, Spain, Germany, the United States, the U.K., Canada, Brazil, Thailand, Japan, Italy, and several other countries. The company depends on a tightly interconnected network of global trading partners for efficient, coordinated operations.

Several years ago, when Michelin moved production capacity to other countries and needed to work more closely with customers in emerging markets, Michelin evaluated several B2B solutions. As explained by Jean-Luc Faye, EDI Manager, they wanted to replace their legacy B2B platform with a modern, scalable B2B infrastructure that would support their complex and growing global operations and provide them with robust security. What follows are excerpts from an interview with Mr. Faye.

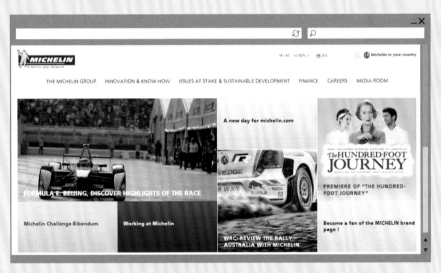

FIGURE 5.10: Michelin - Operational Excellence with B2B Managed Services

"Michelin had a legacy B2B platform which was completely obsolete. Our operations were becoming increasingly global in nature. We were dealing with ever-increasing exchange protocols, messaging standards, and security standards. We were introduced to the concept of Managed Services, in which our B2B Infrastructure would be fully outsourced, hosted in the cloud, and day-to-day operations would be managed for us. The Trading Grid and B2B Managed Services had great appeal to us and completely aligned with our B2B strategy for standardization, fast deployment, and support for future growth. We embarked on a journey in this direction and we have been extremely happy with the outcome.

Managed Services experts performed all activities such as mapping, connectivity, onboarding, testing, monitoring, and end-user support. With all required technology hosted in an integration cloud, we did not have to invest

93

in software or hardware. We started with 500 trading partners, but today this network has expanded to include 750 trading partners. We're continually expanding. There's no place in the world where we are not making new connections. The managed service has provided exceptional management of our mission-critical operations. It is flexible, scalable, and secure.

Michelin has been using the e-Invoicing solution to process more than 1,200 invoices every single day. In the last year, we have processed nearly one million invoices with customers in France and Spain. Today, we have a scalable, modern, B2B platform. Managed Services has enabled us to extend the number of protocols that we support, including any-to-any protocol and any-to-any format. Other benefits include enhanced supply chain monitoring, reporting, and visibility—capabilities that are incredibly important to us.

By outsourcing our EDI, Michelin has offloaded the complexity of day-to-day operations. In return, my team has been able to focus more closely on managing our business operations, achieving business excellence, and working with EDI and B2B integrators to help them better understand the business. This is truly a win-win situation that benefits the business, makes us more efficient and cost effective, and provides us with flexibility and scalability to support our global operations both now and in the years ahead."

Layering Value to Create Business Networks

Recent innovations in SCM have expanded B2B integration networks with the addition of value-chain support services in a managed-service business environment. Many organizations are opting for an outsourced, SaaS, or Platform-as-a-Service (PaaS) managed-service approach for their B2B integration activities to reduce the complexities of connecting with partners, support multiple information exchange protocols, and deal with messaging and security standards.

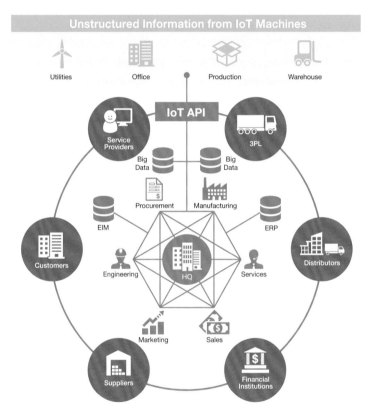

FIGURE 5.11: The Business Network

As organizations depend on third parties to oversee all their day-to-day transactions, the B2B integration network is being layered with more value. Solutions for BPM, EIM, and big data analytics add value to networks. At the same time, the types of information flowing over the network are expanding to include faxes, email, Short Message Service (SMS), and voice data alongside traditional EDI transactions. B2B integration gives organizations the ability to build a broad B2B network that connects transactions, process collaboration, payments, information, and business intelligence.[27]

Incredible value can be derived by collecting, managing, and analyzing information from various business applications across the network. As a platform for the digital enterprise, EIM can provide new intelligence for a multitude of purposes beyond optimizing the supply chain. Integrating the following technologies controls the flow of information across the enterprise with partners, suppliers, and customers each adding a layer of value to the ecosystem:

1. **EIM** - Both unstructured and structured information flows across the extended enterprise. EIM consolidates all information for a single version of the truth, uniting front- and back-office systems based on ERP to manage information transparently and securely throughout its lifecycle.

2. **B2B Integration** - Companies need to connect to a variety of external trading partners using many different communication protocols and document standards. B2B integration capabilities and the Trading Grid provide these capabilities. EIM capabilities can then be applied to manage and secure data exchanged between trading partners.

3. **IoT Networks** - As devices, machines, and sensors connect to the Internet, they will need to exchange big data and information with the digital enterprise.

4. **Internal Systems** - In order to integrate information from IoT devices into back-end enterprise systems, information will need to be exchanged through dedicated Application Programming Interfaces (APIs). Many APIs are currently in development, and in the near future, they will be available for integration with B2B, ERP, and other systems.

The combined end result is a comprehensive and automated platform for the management and exchange of supply chain information. EIM is a platform that enables and empowers both users and technology to produce, access, and consume information with a secure and managed approach. Using EIM as a common platform, the digital supply chain becomes empowered to connect, collaborate, and re-invent itself to lead in 2020.

---

[27] Bob Ferrari, "GXS-The Hidden Gem in B2B Information Services and Application Support", The Ferrari Consulting and Research Group LLC and the Supply Chain Matters Blog, June 14, 2012, http://www.theferrarigroup.com/supply-chain-matters/2012/06/14/gxs-the-hidden-gem-in-b2b-information-services-and-application-support/ (accessed July 2012).

The Digital Supply Chain: A Strategic Imperative

In a digital-first world, companies will depend on supply chain operations to deliver a superior customer experience. Supply chain excellence is strategic to the success of the digital business, but incredibly challenging in today's evolving business environment. Supply chains must rapidly respond to changing service expectations of customers, accommodate a new cycle of frequent product introductions and promotional offers, cope with exploding volumes of cross-border trade, and operate seamlessly and efficiently within a fragmented, global ecosystem of partners and suppliers—all while maintaining profitability and service levels.

While the new environment provides exciting ways of engaging customers and opportunities for revenue growth, it is also requiring companies to radically change or, in many cases, completely overhaul their supply chain processes. As companies specialize and outsource, their operations need to scale, shift, and contract depending on business and market requirements. New channels need to be leveraged and new markets need to be serviced.

Increased flexibility and agility is the key to success, and companies are achieving this by digitizing core business processes and adopting emerging technologies for increased flexibility, cost savings, and improved performance. Today's leading organizations are assembling service processes rapidly with SPAs, automating service processes with DCM, and delivering 24/7 engagement with self-service capabilities. B2B integration is providing sophisticated synchronization of data and transactions for the automated exchange of goods, commerce, and information. Sensors and RFID are increasing the tagging and tracking of inventory. End-to-end supply chain visibility is providing incredible insights for supply chain optimization. The IoT is enhancing the richness of supply chain information creating value chains that are intelligent and instrumented. Managing all of this information across a collaborative platform is the key to supply chain optimization and for exchanging information in efficient, secure, and compliant ways.

To meet the challenges of the digital supply chain, the digital enterprise will depend on digital technology for increased global collaboration, seamless communication, real-time insights, and action. The digital workplace will have to accommodate these shifts in the market and provide the technical expertise required to manage disruptive innovations, optimize a digital supply chain, and satisfy customers to drive competitive advantage. This evolution is the focus of the next chapter on the Digital Workplace.

THE DIGITAL WORKPLACE

CHAPTER 6
The Digital Workplace

"By 2020, we believe people supply will be the most critical driving factor for business success. Companies may go to extreme lengths in their search for talent and, once they have it, they will take measures to keep people 'locked in' to their organizations. Without this talent, they will be unable to compete."[1]

As the business world emerges from a period of economic uncertainty, business leaders are setting positive growth expectations. After years of cost cutting, they are viewing investment in talent as fundamental to meeting growth objectives and increasing competitiveness. In a study of executives that spans 20 countries and 12 industries, over 75 percent of those surveyed plan to scale up their investments in human capital, with 65 percent planning to expand their workforce in the coming year.[2]

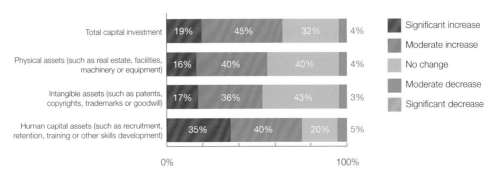

FIGURE 6.1: Increased Investment in Human Capital[3]

These business leaders are ramping up for a disruptive future. In 2020, they will need to be prepared by having the right skill sets in place to manage and optimize disruptive technologies for competitive advantage. Both are top of mind: when executives were asked to identify ways to improve competitiveness, a well-trained workforce (30 percent) and the adoption of new technologies to drive productivity (29 percent) topped the list (see Figure 6.2). In 2020, business leaders will need to create a work environment that embraces digital technology and incorporates modern employment practices to empower employees as the engine for growth and competitive advantage.

---

[1] *"CEO Briefing 2014: The Global Agenda: Competing in a Digital World"*, Accenture, 2014, *http://www.accenture.com/ SiteCollectionDocuments/PDF/Accenture-Global-Agenda-CEO-Briefing-2014-Competing-Digital-World.pdf* (accessed July, 2014).

[2] Ibid.

[3] Ibid.

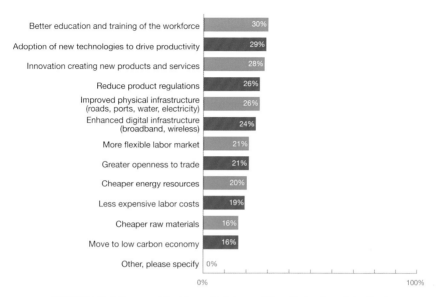

FIGURE 6.2: A Focus on Workforce Training and New Technology Adoption[4]

A Global, Shifting Workforce

Executives will need to attract and retain top talent to achieve their goals and objectives. They will need to create a work environment that appeals to job applicants and, once employed, keeps them productive and engaged. But, the employment landscape is in flux—impacted by a confluence of disruptive forces that are transforming the workplace and changing the nature of work. Among the most powerful of these disruptive forces are digital technologies, globalization, and shifting demographics in the workplace. We will discuss each factor in turn.

Digital technologies are already creating a world that is increasingly interconnected and interdependent. By the year 2020, open communication platforms, collaborative technologies, video conferencing, sophisticated machine-language translation technologies, and even holographic technology will fuel a global workplace by enabling zero-distance communications. As the lines continue to blur between professional and private lives, the workplace will have to support new ways to collaborate. A future, tech-savvy workforce will be self-empowered with consumer technologies like social media, mobile connectivity, gesture-based interfaces, and wearable devices.[5] A digital workplace will be required to transform the employee experience.

[4] "CEO Briefing 2014: The Global Agenda: Competing in a Digital World", Accenture, 2014, http://www.accenture.com/SiteCollectionDocuments/PDF/Accenture-Global-Agenda-CEO-Briefing-2014-Competing-Digital-World.pdf (accessed July, 2014).

[5] Jean-Pierre Garbani, "Prepare for 2020: Transform Your IT Infrastructure and Operations Practice", Forrester Research, October 24, 2012.

Globalization and the growth of emerging markets are also impacting today's work environment. The flow of wealth into countries like China and India has produced robust economies bolstered by a strong middle-class. Momentum continues in their favor: a second wave of globalization is supplanting developed nations in both the U.S. and Europe as the dominant contributors to global economic growth.[6] Organizations in developing regions are expanding their operations and extending their recruitment efforts beyond their local ecosystems. As a result, the 2020 workplace will be more diverse and sophisticated, bringing together different languages, cultures, and ways of working. Business leaders will need to create and nurture a work environment that is multicultural and cosmopolitan. New rules of engagement will be defined to accommodate a complex set of employee needs and expectations for the workplace.

The Multi-Generation Workforce

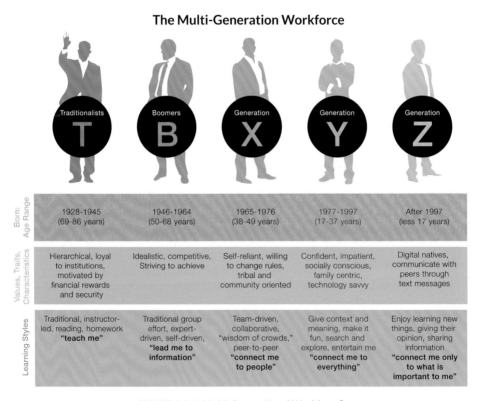

Born: Age Range	1928-1945 (69-86 years)	1946-1964 (50-68 years)	1965-1976 (38-49 years)	1977-1997 (17-37 years)	After 1997 (less 17 years)
Values, Traits, Characteristics	Hierarchical, loyal to institutions, motivated by financial rewards and security	Idealistic, competitive, Striving to achieve	Self-reliant, willing to change rules, tribal and community oriented	Confident, impatient, socially conscious, family centric, technology savvy	Digital natives, communicate with peers through text messages
Learning Styles	Traditional, instructor-led, reading, homework **"teach me"**	Traditional group effort, expert-driven, self-driven, **"lead me to information"**	Team-driven, collaborative, "wisdom of crowds," peer-to-peer **"connect me to people"**	Give context and meaning, make it fun, search and explore, entertain me **"connect me to everything"**	Enjoy learning new things, giving their opinion, sharing information **"connect me only to what is important to me"**

FIGURE 6.3: A Multi-Generational Workforce[7]

[6] *"Transitioning to Workforce 2020"*, Cisco, 2011, *http://www.cisco.com/web/learning/employer_resources/pdfs/ Workforce_2020_White_Paper.pdf* (accessed July 2014).

[7] Bersin, Josh, *"A New Organizational Learning Model: Learning On-Demand"*, Bersin by Deloitte, October 1, 2007, *http://joshbersin.com/2007/10/a-new-organizational-learning-model-learning-on-demand/* (accessed September 2014).

Global changes in demographics are also creating a more complex workforce. The 2020 workforce is both shrinking and aging, and this will result in a sizable reduction in working populations over the next 50 years.[8] A global study revealed that large numbers of prospective retirees plan to delay retirement in Australia (44 percent), the U.S. (40 percent), Mexico (36 percent), France (28 percent) and the UK (23 percent).[9] While some retirees in these countries will remain in the workforce because they want to continue working, the majority will continue to work out of financial necessity.

The most notable impact of demographics on the digital workplace will be its requirement to support multiple generations in its workforce: Traditionalists, Baby Boomers, Generation X, Generation Y, and Generation Z. For the first time in history, organizations will be tasked with managing the very divergent needs and expectations of these five demographic groups. The younger generations will bring digital disruption and new ways to work into the workforce. The older generations will take their knowledge and expertise with them when they leave. Both will need access to integrated technologies and approaches to working that facilitate knowledge exchange.

1. Traditionalists

Traditionalists (born before 1946) are the senior generation in the 2020 workplace. They are hardworking, dependable, and loyal employees who tend to put their personal needs aside for the greater good. While the tail end of this generation will be 75 years old by 2020, many will postpone their retirement to remain in the workforce.[10]

2. Baby Boomers

Baby Boomers (born between 1946 and 1964) have dominated the workforce for many years and are approaching retirement. Boomers have a strong work ethic and a deep loyalty to a single employer. In return for their loyalty, they expect to climb the corporate ladder and be well compensated. Many in this generation are choosing to delay retirement. When surveyed, half of all working adults in the U.S. today between 50 and 64 say they will delay retirement and another 16 percent report that they never expect to stop working.[11]

---

[8] Jeanne C. Meister & Karie Willyerd, *"The 2020 Workplace"*, HarperCollins Publishers, 2010.

[9] Daniel W. Rasmus, *"Global Trend 6: Fostering a Global Workforce in Dynamic Times"*, Ernst & Young, *http://www.ey.com/GL/en/Issues/Business-environment/Business-redefined---Global-trend-6--Fostering-a-global-workforce-in-dynamic-times* (accessed July 2014).

[10] Jeanne C. Meister & Karie Willyerd, *"The 2020 Workplace"*, HarperCollins Publishers, 2010.

[11] Ibid.

3. Generation X

Generation X refers to those born between 1965 and 1976. The attitudes of this generation are markedly different from earlier generations. Many in this generation began their careers in a period of social and economic change. Gen Xers are mercenary in nature and place a greater emphasis on achieving a work/life balance than financial success[12]. As the Baby Boomers retire, Gen X will mentor the next generation: Generation Y.

4. Generation Y

Generation Y (born between 1977 and 1997) are the first half of the Millennial Generation. They have boundless ambition, optimism, and self-confidence. The rise of the World Wide Web occurred during their formative years and they began using the Internet, mobile devices, and social platforms as children. Today, they are a digitally savvy group that is adaptable to technology in the workplace. This generation wants to work for an organization that does something they believe in, supports their desire to learn and acquire new skills, allows them to be self-directed, and empowers them to make a difference in the world.

5. Generation Z

Generation Z (born after 1997 as the latter half of the Millennial Generation) is considered to be the "Net Generation". Gen Z takes the hyper-connectivity of Gen Y to new levels. Technology plays a central role in their lives; they have used it since toddlerhood for homework and to communicate with peers. Nearly one in four (or 25 percent) connect within five minutes of waking up (reading email, text messaging, etc.), while three in four connect within an hour or less. And while a full 100 percent are connected for one hour a day; nearly half are connected ten or more hours a day.[13] Their use of technology sets Generation Z apart from other generations, and they will bring this with them into any workplace. When combined with innovative technologies, Generation Z could very well be the greatest disruptors of the enterprise and current ways of working.

Catering to the Expectations of Generation Z

Generation Z represents the greatest generational shift the workplace has ever seen. In 2020, they will make up almost 50 percent of the global workforce.[14] Because they inherently understand and rely on digital technology, they will play a critical role in shaping the digital workplace.

---

[12] Jeanne C. Meister & Karie Willyerd, *"The 2020 Workplace"*, HarperCollins Publishers, 2010.

[13] *"Millennials at Work Reshaping the Workplace"* PriceWaterhouseCoopers, 2011, *http://www.pwc.com/en_M1/m1/services/consulting/documents/millennials-at-work.pdf* (accessed July 2014).

[14] Michael Scaduto, *"Make Way for Generation Z"* In Context Magazine, December 9, 2013, *http://www.incontextmag.com/articles/2013/make-way-for-generation-z.html* (accessed July 2014).

Generation Z is the "digital elite", and employers will need to cater to their expectations to attract and retain them in 2020. As they enter the workforce, Generation Z will expect to use the same tools in the office that they use in their leisure time—tools for instant connection and immediate response, easy and effective collaboration, and fast and easy access to information. If the newest technologies are not provided, they will either bring disruptive devices and applications inside the firewall or find a new place to work.

Generation Z will require employers to create a work environment that supports their work ethic. Transparency, self-reliance, flexibility, and personal freedom are non-negotiable aspects of the Generation Z work ethic.[15] How does this translate into working conditions? The 2020 workplace will be required to adopt digital technologies to empower employees to work in ways that are open, flexible, and fast. As a group they will present profound challenges to leaders and Human Resources (HR) managers and initiate digital transformation.

New Job Requirements

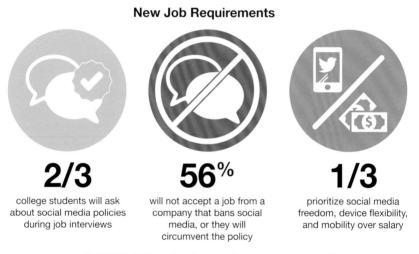

2/3
college students will ask about social media policies during job interviews

56%
will not accept a job from a company that bans social media, or they will circumvent the policy

1/3
prioritize social media freedom, device flexibility, and mobility over salary

FIGURE 6.4: Workplace Expectations for Generation Z[16]

[15] Michael Scaduto, *"Make Way for Generation Z"* In Context Magazine, December 9, 2013, *http://www.incontextmag.com/articles/2013/make-way-for-generation-z.html* (accessed July 2014).

[16] *"Millennials at Work Reshaping the Workplace"* PriceWaterhouseCoopers, 2011, *http://www.pwc.com/en_M1/m1/services/consulting/documents/millennials-at-work.pdf* (accessed July 2014).

Building the Digital Workplace

The digital workplace is a work environment that supports new ways of working, based on integrated applications that make employees more efficient and productive. These tools run the gamut, from intranets and portals to social networks and mobile devices, crowdsourcing, gamification, holographic images—and for 2020 digital employees, technologies that have not yet been conceived. The digital enterprise will need to provide rapid access to emerging technologies to facilitate collaboration, knowledge sharing, and communication in unprecedented ways. A key differentiator for the 2020 workplace is that digital technologies will help to create an environment that is flexible, mobile, social, collaborative, and innovative. The digital enterprise will be required to stay on top of emerging trends and new technologies to support its digital workplace.

"If you understand the Net Generation, you will understand the future. You will also understand how our institutions and society need to change today."[17]

Organizational Structures Are Flat and Decentralized

Digital technologies will help to transform the traditional hierarchies and structure of the enterprise. When interviewed, 65 percent of younger generations felt that rigid hierarchies and outdated management styles failed to get the most out of younger recruits.[18] Many anticipate a massive shift from a command-and-control to a coordinate-and-cultivate organizational structure. In 2020, a flattening of hierarchies, decentralization of control, and the emergence of cross-functional teams will give individual workers greater autonomy.

The new decentralized enterprise will apply digital technology to create a dynamic, fluid infrastructure that can form and reform according to current needs, using contractors, consultants, and vendors located around the world. In the digital workplace, self-service capabilities will become extremely important as direct ways to access information and resources and technology will facilitate this.[19] Digital employees will expect to manage their own profiles with personal information, access a pay stub, complete expense reports, or find information about a health benefit in a fully integrated workspace.

---

[17] *"CEO Briefing 2014: The Global Agenda: Competing in a Digital World"*, Accenture, 2014, http://www.accenture.com/SiteCollectionDocuments/PDF/Accenture-Global-Agenda-CEO-Briefing-2014-Competing-Digital-World.pdf (accessed July, 2014).

[18] *"Transitioning to Workforce 2020"*, Cisco, 2011, http://www.cisco.com/web/learning/employer_resources/pdfs/Workforce_2020_White_Paper.pdf (accessed July 2014).

[19] Michael Scaduto, *"Make Way for Generation Z"* In Context Magazine, December 9, 2013, http://www.incontextmag.com/articles/2013/make-way-for-generation-z.html (accessed July 2014).

The digital workplace will allow for more freedom and control. Studies of Research and Development (R&D) projects have found that when the members of project teams feel more freedom and control over their work, they become more innovative. When people make their own decisions about how to do their work and allocate their time, they often put more energy, effort, and creativity into their jobs.[20]

Remote and Mobile Access

There is growing evidence that employees are more productive if they have greater autonomy over where, when, and how they work. The digital workplace will provide employees with tools and information to work in ways that are flexible, open, and self-service in nature.

Younger generations prefer flexible work arrangements over the traditional office environment.[21] In one survey, three out of five employees do not believe they have to work in an office to be productive, 66 percent want flexibility in how they work and would accept a lower-paying job it if meant more flexibility, and a significant portion of employees regard working from home as a right rather than a privilege (see Figure 6.5 below).[22]

In 2020, the digital enterprise will have fewer on-site employees and leaner headquarter facilities. Workers will be organized into global teams formed around expertise; they will not report to offices or keep set hours. A wide range of digital technologies will facilitate this global, virtual workforce.

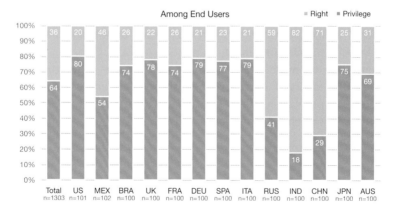

FIGURE 6.5: Working Remotely - A Right or a Privilege?[23]

[20] Michael Scaduto, *"Make Way for Generation Z" In Context Magazine*, December 9, 2013, *http://www.incontextmag.com/articles/2013/make-way-for-generation-z.html* (accessed July 2014).

[21] *"Transitioning to Workforce 2020"*, Cisco, 2011, *http://www.cisco.com/web/learning/employer_resources/pdfs/Workforce_2020_White_Paper.pdf* (accessed July 2014).

[22] Ibid.

[23] Ibid.

The 2020 workplace will be made up of mobile workforce. Most organizations, 88 percent according to one study, are already offering their workforce personal devices such as smartphones, PDAs, and tablets.[24] Digital technologies link physical devices with virtual and mobile environments to facilitate the transparent exchange of information. Mobile devices connect mobile professionals with content, processes, and resources in their preferred environment for access from any place at any time to optimize productivity.

Even today, an increasing number of employees are bringing their own mobile devices to work, regardless of whether or not there is a formal Bring-Your-Own-Device (BYOD) policy in place. In the U.S., employees currently pay for over 40 percent of the devices and data plans used for work, and they pay for 70 percent of the tablets used for work.[25] Combining personal and work information on a device, however, presents serious security threats to the organization. As the digital enterprise embraces mobile devices and tablets, or as wearable devices make their way into the workplace, security will be a growing concern. This is discussed in the following chapter on Digital Governance.

A Highly Social, Collaborative Workplace

Younger generations of workers will expect a workplace ecosystem that is highly social and collaborative. A recent report found that two thirds of current college students plan to ask about social media policies during job interviews, and 56 percent say they will not accept a job from a company that bans social media or, if they do, they will find ways to circumvent policies.[26]

In 2020, the digital workplace will provide a seamless and rich collaborative experience. Social networking, instant messaging, video-on-demand, blogs, and wikis will dominate communications. Unlike an intranet, which is typically organized by function or role, a digital workplace is socially-enabled, facilitating knowledge exchange according to areas of expertise or by project. Social technologies foster the natural formation of communities around topics of interest. Within these communities, tools like wikis and blogs can be used to provide employees with a platform for exchanging and managing workplace conversations and information.

[24] Ramez T. Shehadi et al, *"Designing the digital workplace: Connectivity, communication, collaboration"*, PriceWaterhouseCoopers, 2013.

[25] *"Prepare for 2020: Transform Your IT Infrastructure and Operations Practice"*, Forrester Research, 2012.

[26] *"Transitioning to Workforce 2020"*, Cisco, 2011, http://www.cisco.com/web/learning/employer_resources/pdfs/Workforce_2020_White_Paper.pdf (accessed July 2014).

When combined, digital tools can transform a corporate intranet into a dynamic and interactive structure built by distributed peers. They can be used to share information, innovate, and crowdsource to solve problems. In addition, as more people author, link, and tag information, an organization's content becomes more searchable, analyzable, and manageable. When the processes around information are seamless and visible, it becomes easier for an organization to meet regulatory requirements. With collaborative capabilities bundled as part of an integrated enterprise information management system, employees are able to access the information and expertise they need to do their jobs— and can freely share ideas and knowledge to innovate in a secure but open environment.

FIGURE 6.6: A Social Community of Practice

More than half of organizations (54 percent) in one study actively use Facebook, LinkedIn®, Twitter®, and other tools to engage their workforce, customers, and other stakeholders.[27] The benefits that social engagement offers include higher levels of productivity and greater employee satisfaction. Empowered employees can connect immediately, exchange information, and participate in conversations in real time. Organizations that make use of social media tools have experienced a 20 percent increase in employee satisfaction, are up to seven percent more productive, and have discovered that when employees are engaged, retention rates increase by as much as 87 percent.[28]

In the following feature, Givaudan is transforming its workplace using social tools like online communities and wikis to bring together its employees to share ideas and best practices, improve productivity, and foster innovation.

[27] Ramez T. Shehadi et al, *"Designing the digital workplace: Connectivity, communication, collaboration"*, PriceWaterhouseCoopers, 2013.

[28] Frederico Herrera, *"The Digital Workplace: Think, share, do"*, Deloitte Canada, 2011.

Givaudan

Givaudan, headquartered in Vernier, Switzerland, is an established leader in the fragrance and flavour industry, boasting over 25 percent in market share and ranking as one of Switzerland's top 30 companies. They are a global company with 9,000 staff located in 80 offices in 40 countries around the world. Over Givaudan's 115 year history, they have grown both organically and through mergers and acquisitions. As a result, they have accumulated a multitude of systems and processes throughout the organization—a situation that has hindered effective information management, sharing, and collaboration. In 2008, Givaudan set out to digitalize their workplace—to provide employees with improved access to information and tools for enhanced workplace collaboration on a global scale. Xavier Ainsiaux, Head of the ECM & Social Collaboration Competence Centre at Givaudan, discussed the company's transformational journey in a recent interview. What follows are some excerpts from the interview.

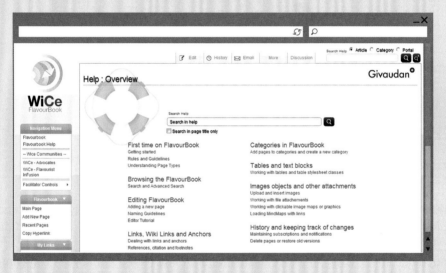

FIGURE 6.7: Givaudan's FlavorBook Wiki

"We always viewed information as an asset. But we had a large number of systems in place and information silos across the organization. The task of making information from across the organization globally accessible and usable was somewhat daunting. We took it one step at a time. Our journey started by centralizing the company's structured data and transactions in an Enterprise Resource Planning (ERP) system. From there, we set out to consolidate transactional data from numerous legacy systems. A huge consolidation and legacy de-commissioning project—which involved 30 factories around the world—produced incredible cost savings and workplace efficiencies.

We wanted to establish a 'single source of the truth' for our unstructured information—for our documentation, presentations, spreadsheets, and more. We had a situation in which files were shared by email attachment and employees had no way to confirm they were working with the latest version. After researching a number of vendors, we implemented a content management solution and rolled it out to all 9,000 Givaudan employees worldwide.

With content stored in a single, central repository, employees can now search for content and, once located, be confident they are looking at the very latest version of the document. Teams can create project folders for their working documents and those assigned access can open and save changes to project documents. This technology has transformed our organization—the way information is managed and the way teams work together on projects. Today, employees in all functional areas use this system. Over the years it has just become the natural place where people go to store documents.

As part of this project, employees in our Flavors and Creation organization were looking to share best practices and collaborate about product formulas. They envisioned using a wiki—a social media tool like Wikipedia—where one person adds an entry and another person builds upon it. By recording their best practices in a wiki— what was tried, what the result was—others in the organization can benefit. In time, when another person needs to create a product, they can go to the wiki, search it, and learn from past experience. And they can build upon it with their own experiences.

Today, the Flavors and Creation wiki, called FlavorBook, has become a hub for research and collaboration in our workplace. Employees have adopted it because it is user friendly. Pages display information with images, whitespace, and navigation in ways that are familiar. Content is searchable and easy to find. The accessibility and usability of the wiki makes employees more efficient and productive. It allows them to collaborate, build their collective knowledge, and use that knowledge to innovate. By managing content effectively and embracing digital tools for collaboration, we have created a work environment that no longer hinders employees but empowers them.

Innovative Models of Engagement

As demonstrated in the feature above, providing unrestricted or open access to information, knowledge, and capabilities helps employees innovate, engage, and contribute in ways not previously possible or imaginable.

Crowdsourcing is an example of this phenomenon. The term "crowdsourcing" was coined by editors Jeff Howe and Mark Robinson at *Wired Magazine* in 2005. It means essentially "outsourcing to the crowd". It occurs when organizations make their information (market data, customer data, product plans, usage patterns, etc.) openly available for citizens, employees, and others to share knowledge and innovate. As part of the open source movement, providing free access to information and digital tools facilitates innovation by giving anyone with the right mindset the capabilities to develop new solutions.

Crowdsourced innovation delivers amazing advantages to the digital enterprise. Consumer goods companies, for example, can increase their speed to market for new products and do so with lower development costs. In many instances, the outcomes are more effective because products are more closely aligned with consumer needs. Today, consumer goods manufacturers spend more than $20 billion annually on R&D. New digital tools and technologies will make it easier and less costly to engage crowds and establish on-demand, high-value connections with them. It is predicted that by 2017, over half of consumer goods manufacturers will employ crowdsourcing to achieve 75 percent of their consumer innovation and R&D capabilities.[29]

FIGURE 6.8: Crowdsourcing in the Digital Enterprise

[29] Frederico Herrera, *"The Digital Workplace: Think, share, do"*, Deloitte Canada, 2011.

Crowdsourcing is currently being applied by governments and not-for-profits as a problem-solving tool for community building, civic engagement, and funding, but it is finding its way inside the firewall. Both the U.S. and Canadian governments are crowdsourcing to improve engagement and performance. The SAVE Award (Securing Americans Value and Efficiency) recognizes U.S. Federal employees for thinking outside the box to make government more efficient and bring value for taxpayer dollars. To date, Federal employees have submitted more than 85,000 ideas, with the most promising ideas included in the President's Budget.[30]

In the private sector, businesses are increasingly accomplishing work through innovative sourcing models to leverage the crowd. Crowdsourcing is a new way of distributing work across functional and departmental teams within an organization. Innovation labs are another disruptive, new approach to teamwork. Typically made up of designated "tiger teams", they function across departmental and even organizational boundaries to brainstorm, research, and solve technical or systemic problems. The past two years has seen an explosion in the use of innovation labs to identify, manage, and select innovation opportunities, and this will only increase as the workplace becomes more collaborative through disruptive technologies. For example, @WalmartLabs is currently focusing on creating the next generation of commerce by combining online, mobile, and retail outlets to let customers shop when, where, and how they want. Their mission is to transform themselves into one of "the top technology companies in Silicon Valley" using their labs to foster innovation and collaboration to create best-in-class e-commerce technologies.[31]

In 2020, the digital workplace will be able to transform any surface into a collaborative workspace. According to experts, by 2025, holographic technology will enable users to invoke workspaces anywhere by using interactive surfaces.[32] Using holographs, designers and developers will be able to touch icons in space and do things like draw in mid-air with the added dimensions of real-space interactivity. Holograph technology will be sold for integration into diverse applications, including medical training, military simulation and situational awareness, 3-D entertainment, and gaming. As holography like this develops, it will not only revolutionize industry, but also how we interact and communicate with each other.

[30] "The President's SAVE Award", The White House, http://www.whitehouse.gov/save-award (accessed February 2014).

[31] Frederico Herrera, "The Digital Workplace: Think, share, do", Deloitte Canada, 2011.

[32] Mark Heraghty, "The workplace of 2025 will be wherever you want it", BBC News, September 2012, http://www.bbc.com/news/business-19639048 (accessed May 2014).

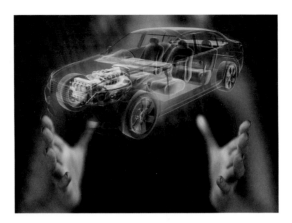

FIGURE 6.9: Holographic Images Take Collaboration to the Next Level

Digital Recruiting and Retention

Digital technology is also having a profound impact on talent management. With increasing reliance on self-service technology, sensors, machine-to-machine communication, and Artificial Intelligence (AI), there will be a shift toward work that is tacit and non-routine—and a shortage of workers with the skills required to fill them.[33] As discussed earlier in Chapter 2, tacit jobs require a complex set of skills such as problem solving, judgment, listening, data analysis, relationship building, and collaborating and communicating with co-workers. Roles that fulfill tacit jobs will increase and change the nature of the workforce.

Based on the anticipated skills shortage and a shrinking pool from which to attract talent, the digital enterprise will compete vigorously to attract employees. In a digital-first world, organizations will need to attract and retain knowledge workers with the skill sets required to manage disruptive technologies. In a recent survey, 35 percent of executives cite skills shortages as the biggest barrier to implementing digital technologies and 60 percent list investments in attracting and retaining the best talent as key to their business.[34] In a digital economy, the nature of work is changing, and it is becoming critical to create a workplace and a work environment that will attract and retain the right talent.

[33] Jeremy Rifkin, *"The Zero Marginal Cost Society"*, St. Martin's Press, 2014.

[34] *"CEO Briefing 2014: The Global Agenda: Competing in a Digital World"*, Accenture, 2014, *http://www.accenture.com/SiteCollectionDocuments/PDF/Accenture-Global-Agenda-CEO-Briefing-2014-Competing-Digital-World.pdf* (accessed July 2014).

In 2020, job seekers will look for employment almost exclusively using social media channels that match job seekers with available opportunities. Sites like LinkedIn, Facebook, and Twitter leverage data analytics to identify compatibilities and suggest pairings. Managing online reputations and profiles will become increasingly important for both corporations and individuals. Video resumes will feature prominently in 2020 recruiting, with 80 percent of employers expecting to use video as a standard tool for recruiting, onboarding, and talent management. A video resume allows recruiters to fast forward through candidates, focus on those with potential, and complete 8 or 9 screenings per hour.[35] As well as adding efficiency and reducing the costs associated with multiple interviews, video resumes can be distributed to other stakeholders in the hiring process to gain buy-in and approval before investing in the in-person interview. While changes to recruiting processes introduce incredible convenience and efficiency, the processes, media, and information will have to be managed securely in the digital workplace.

Once the right employees are attracted, the digital workplace will be tasked with retaining their top talent by offering exceptional training and career development programs. To be effective, many of these programs will incorporate learning into social media, gaming, real-time feedback, and simulations.[36]

Gamification is a growing trend in the field of learning and involves using gaming elements to teach a concept. Gamification presents users with an immersive (and typically social) experience that deepens their engagement, which in turn increases user adoption to achieve a business objective. As the gaming industry grows, the enterprise will adopt gamification techniques to gamify programs, websites, processes, and applications. Gamification techniques work well in an enterprise setting and can result in higher levels of employee satisfaction, improved performance, enhanced collaboration and team building, and increased innovation and ideation.

Reciprocal mentoring is also a notable trend worth mentioning in the field of learning and development, and one that is favored by Generation Z (see Figure 6.10). For reciprocal mentoring, members of different generations are paired and provide the other with complementary knowledge. Older employees share what they know about the industry, how the organization works, how to navigate office politics, and how to do specific jobs—based on years of experience. The younger generations share their knowledge of digital technology. A member of Generation Z, for example, would teach a Baby Boomer how to create a profile on Facebook or YouTube or upload images to Instagram. In the process of reciprocal mentoring, relationships are built, generations share knowledge and experience, and each gains a better understanding of the values the other brings to the organization. Both require the effective management of information to facilitate secure and accurate knowledge sharing.

[35] Michael Scaduto, "Make Way for Generation Z" In Context Magazine, December 9, 2013, http://www.incontextmag.com/articles/2013/make-way-for-generation-z.html (accessed July 2014).

[36] Jeanne C. Meister & Karie Willyerd, "The 2020 Workplace", HarperCollins Publishers, 2010.

FIGURE 6.10: A Preference for Mentors[37]

Preparing Today for the Workplace of Tomorrow

The collaborative model of the digital workplace will revolutionize job functions, management methods, lines of authority, and employee expectations.[38] Although this is just around the corner, many organizations will fail to reinvent themselves as a digital workplace because of poorly integrated information and processes, communication silos, inadequate mobile and BYOD programs, and an inability to leverage consumer technologies securely inside the firewall.

The new generations of employees are smart and savvy and they understand how digital technology can deliver competitive advantage. They expect to use these technologies to help them create and innovate. Leading organizations are already preparing their digital strategies to win the quest for top talent. They are embracing disruptive technologies and modernizing their HR practices. They are consolidating the technologies that promote an open, flexible, mobile, social, and innovative workplace on a proven Enterprise Information Management (EIM) platform. The digital workplace will create volumes of data and information. Beyond setting a strategy for digital transformation and putting the appropriate digital tools in place, the enterprise will face many challenges in the areas of compliance, governance, and risk.

Globalization, digital technology, demographic changes, and the changing expectations of new generations are converging to produce the digital workplace. They will put pressure on the organization to adapt and evolve. When creating a digital workplace, organizations must implement an infrastructure that supports connectivity and collaboration while enabling compliance. Information governance will be a key requirement in 2020 and is explored in the following chapter.

[37] "Millennials at Work Reshaping the Workplace", PriceWaterhouseCoopers, 2011,
http://www.pwc.com/en_M1/m1/services/consulting/documents/millennials-at-work.pdf (accessed July 2014).

[38] "Transitioning to Workforce 2020", Cisco, 2011,
http://www.cisco.com/web/learning/employer_resources/pdfs/Workforce_2020_White_Paper.pdf (accessed July 2014).

DIGITAL GOVERNANCE

CHAPTER 7
Digital Governance

"By as early as 2016, 20 percent of CIOs in regulated industries will lose their jobs for failing to implement the discipline of information governance successfully."[1]

As the new currency in a digital-first world, information is a primary driver of transformation and performance. Disruptive technologies will contribute to the creation, distribution, and fragmentation of enterprise information. In 2020, the Internet of Things (IoT) alone will introduce a wave of new data into the enterprise. The additional volumes of new data types will require that the enterprise be prepared to govern this information before it arrives.

If information is to be an agent of change, it has to be managed. Executives and IT leaders will be required to develop and execute strategies for information management, including robust capabilities for Governance, Risk, and Compliance (GRC). Strategies for managing GRC will help the digital enterprise maximize the value of its information, while minimizing risk. For many organizations, finding this balance will be critical for survival.

Researchers predict that the market for GRC solutions will grow to $10 billion by as early as 2018.[2] As a sustainable platform for GRC, Enterprise Information Management (EIM) arms the strategic CIO and empowers the digital enterprise to put policies and controls in place to address compliance issues, while making critical information available to improve performance and deliver competitive advantage.

A Disruptive Governance Landscape

In every industry, organizations are under increasing levels of scrutiny. In response to recent food-safety issues, the mortgage crisis, and national toy recalls, organizations are stepping up their efforts to improve the management of information that supports key regulatory processes. Externally, the flow of new rules and regulations across regional, national, and international borders continues to intensify. Internally, information is impacted by Corporate Social Responsibility (CSR) pressures. How a company manages its operations and its information has a direct impact on profit and shareholder value. Poor management and non-compliance can lead to lost business, financial penalties, and even criminal charges.

---

[1] Bill O'Kane and Andrew White, et al., *"Predicts 2012: Information Governance and MDM Programs Gain Traction"*, Gartner Inc., *http://www.gartner.com/id=1856616* (accessed 12 Jul. 2013).

[2] *"Enterprise Governance, Risk and Compliance Markets"*, MarketsandMarkets, 2014, *http://www.newportconsgroup.com/wp/wp-content/uploads/Brochure-Enterprise-Governance-Risk-and-Compliance-Market2013-2018-Primary.pdf* (accessed July 2014).

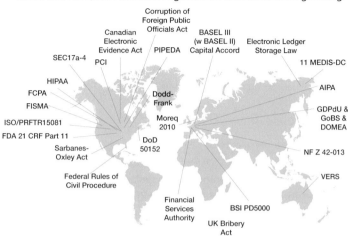

FIGURE 7.1: Global Regulatory Pressures

New and disruptive technologies are also introducing concerns about fraud, ethical behavior, and data security to the enterprise. With the proliferation of big data, social media, cloud computing, and Bring-Your-Own-Device (BYOD) policies around mobile device usage, governance has become a major concern for those responsible for the regulatory and legal ramifications of related technologies and trends—from the CIO to legal counsel to records managers.

Connecting information, people, and processes across the IoT will also present information governance challenges for the enterprise. In most countries, new data types will be subject to regulations. Organizations will need to determine if information is subject to privacy legislation (and cannot be shared or resold without the user's permission) to comply with data protection regulations. The impact of regulations will have far-reaching consequences on many businesses with global office locations and a dispersed workforce.

Many organizations have minimal control over their operational systems and business processes that capture data required for compliance and litigation purposes. For large companies, governance is a major issue, given the complexity of information systems across many departments. In all industries, organizations have made progress in improving the controls required to tap into their mountains of information. But in light of changes to come, there is still work to be done. Digital governance puts processes and controls in place to give full visibility into how information flows throughout an organization. An integrated approach to managing information provides effective solutions for GRC.

By 2020, IT budgets will have to significantly increase to meet the current and future governance and compliance requirements. The majority of financial institutions (61 percent), for example, expect to increase their IT investment by 25 percent in the next three years to comply with regulations.[3] But digital governance goes beyond controlling regulatory information, and when implemented correctly, it uncovers the value of information in its many formats for improved operational performance.

Good Governance Is Good Business

As volumes of enterprise information increase, so too does the need for digital governance to ensure that this information is managed, secured, and searchable. Poor information access can impair the business and systems that rely on paper are a prime example of this. When information is dispersed and copied across many environments, it is harder to share and can hinder processes. There is value in understanding data and turning content into meaningful enterprise information that can be used to optimize the business.

Information governance is the practice of implementing policies, processes, and controls to manage information in support of regulatory, legal, risk, environmental, and operational requirements. From a technology perspective, governance relies on integrated electronic records management, archiving, e-discovery, and storage optimization.[4] These technologies are applied to manage information throughout its lifecycle, from creation or capture and classification to long-term archival or deletion.

Information governance is more than just "records management": It is a means to manage risk, ensure compliance, and achieve operational excellence and competitive advantage from enterprise information.

Successful information governance programs demand that companies balance the needs and priorities to mitigate legal and business risks with the costs required to manage both unstructured and structured information. For a formal strategy for digital governance to be effective, key resources and stakeholders need to be identified, empowered, and supported; policies must be incorporated into relevant processes; education and training should be provided to all employees; technology infrastructure optimized; and the appropriate solutions implemented to support secure and reliable operations.

---

[3] John Ginovsky, *"Compliance needs tech booster"*, ABA Banking Journal, July 21, 2014,
  http://www.ababj.com/blogs-3/making-sense-of-it-all/item/4774-compliance-needs-tech-booster (accessed July 2014).

[4] Alys Woodward and Carla Arend, *"OpenText in Europe: Information Governance and Cultural Transformation"*, IDC, April 22, 2014.

The Stakeholders of Information Stewardship

For proven success, governance strategies must consider the contrasting ways in which information stakeholders view corporate information. For business stakeholders, content is an important means to drive profitability. Their chief concerns are productivity, integration with key processes, information access, knowledge reuse, and time to market. For IT stakeholders, content must be managed efficiently. Their focus is on storage optimization, backup and restore procedures, security, encryption, information lifecycle management, and vendor flexibility. Legal stakeholders regard content in terms of the potential risk it may pose to the enterprise. They strive to put airtight policies and controls in place to ensure that compliance, centralized policy management, discovery and holds, early case assessment, and defensible disposition of content are all working in harmony to mitigate as much risk as possible for the organization.

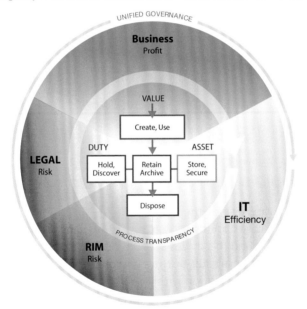

Information Governance Reference Model (IGRM)

Linking duty + value to information asset = efficient, effective management

Duty: Legal Obligation for specific information

Value: Utility or business purpose of specific information

Asset: Specific container of information

FIGURE 7.2: Information Governance Reference Model[5]

[5] EDRM: *http://www.edrm.net/projects/igrm* (accessed July 2014).

Further complicating effective governance is the fact that content is created, modified, and stored by thousands of information workers across multiple business contexts. As depicted in the Information Governance Reference Model (IGRM) above, it is challenging for organizations to align stakeholders and properly address the competing priorities of these constituencies.

Drivers for Digital Governance

In response to these stakeholder needs, many executives are placing greater importance on information governance. Almost two thirds of respondents in a recent survey believe that an information governance program is somewhat or very important to their organizations.[6] The same survey revealed that large organizations in highly regulated sectors, such as defense and aerospace, financial services, and health care, consider information governance to be very important to their business.[7] The more data an organization stores and manages, the greater the risks for security breaches and non compliance.

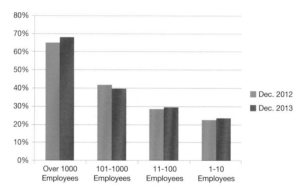

FIGURE 7.3: Importance of Information Governance Based on Company Size[8]

Despite the growing awareness of the importance of governance, organizations are often caught unaware in cases of litigation or non-compliance. Typically, a compelling event impacts the business and this drives stakeholders to take action. When they find themselves faced with a major lawsuit or the e-discovery process, organizations often struggle to identify critical information within their systems. Sorting through volumes of information for relevant records can lead to excessive spending on legal reviews and, in many cases, fines related to the inability to defensibly demonstrate that information has been produced in a timely manner. The same can be true of an investigation related to a regulatory audit. When an organization has faced one of these situations, the cost and business disruptions are often the drivers of governance initiatives.

[6] David Horrigan and Alan Pelz-Sharpe, "451 Data: Information governance falls flat despite the hype", 451 Research, February 20, 2014.

[7] Ibid.

[8] Ibid.

Regulatory Compliance as a Key Driver

Regulatory compliance is the most significant driver of an information governance program. Up to 70 percent of data management professionals consider compliance a critical or high priority.[9] However, organizations that adopt information governance experience additional benefits, including business continuity, savings on storage and infrastructure, unimpeded knowledge sharing, stronger security and privacy, and the ability to respond quickly and proactively to investigations of all types.[10]

FIGURE 7.4: Compliance is Key Driver for Information Governance[11]

For organizations in all sectors, there are complex regulatory and legislative mandates that dictate the way organizations manage their business content. Examples of these include the following:

- **Protection and preservation of content** – In some industries, information must be kept (archived) for 50 or 100 years.

- **Defensible deletion of information** – Some content, such as personnel data, that is related to an incident can fall under defensible deletion within defined timelines.

- **Specific Records Management regulations** – Some regions have different regulations based on very lengthy and complex implementation and feature requirements and specifications.

- **Privacy regulations** – These exist in most regions with increased oversight over types of information stored by organizations, what is shared, and where information is stored. An increasing reliance on cloud computing is causing scrutiny and extensions of this type of regulation requiring organizations to ensure information is kept within specific geographical regions.

[9] Michele Goetz and Henry Peyret, et al., *"Data Governance Equals Business Opportunity. No, Really"*, Forrester Research, *http://www.forrester.com/Data+Governance+Equals+Business+Opportunity+No+Really/fulltext/-/E-RES83342* (accessed May 2013).

[10] Ibid.

[11] Ibid.

No matter how large or diversified an organization is, many aspects of it are caught up in a net of evolving regulations, making the digital enterprise subject to enforcement, hefty fines, and in some cases, reputational risk.

The Benefits Outweigh the Costs

"I didn't know..."

– KEN LAY, FORMER CEO, ENRON

With enforcement, fines, and business reputation at stake, the cost of non-compliance clearly outweighs the cost of investing in digital governance. A recent study of 160 business leaders at 46 multinational companies revealed that the cost of compliance was more than $3.5 million, significantly less than the $9.4 million in estimated costs for failing to comply with regulations.[12]

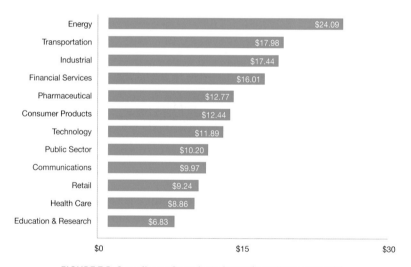

FIGURE 7.5: Compliance Costs by Industry (in Millions of USD)[13]

Non-compliance costs are the costs that result when an organization fails to comply with rules, regulations, policies, contracts, and other legal obligations. On average, companies budget about $1.5 million to comply with laws and regulations.[14] Compliance costs are based on activities that organizations use to meet specific rules, regulations, policies, and contracts that are intended to protect information assets.

[12] *"The True Cost of Compliance"*, Ponemon Institute, January 2011, *http://www.tripwire.com/tripwire/assets/File/ponemon/ True_Cost_of_Compliance_Report.pdf* (accessed July 2014).

[13] Ibid.

[14] Ibid.

There are greater benefits associated with compliance beyond mitigating risk and avoiding penalties. In theory, if an organization is complying with regulations, it should also be achieving higher levels of efficiency and performance through effective information governance. Companies that are not complying with regulations are often paying for business disruption and productivity losses. Regulations are based on demands that describe optimal business operations. By practicing active compliance, organizations are ensuring that their businesses adhere to industry-established best practices and procedures. Compliance gives organizations the mandate to take measures that can uncover value—proactive measures like best practices, employee training, internal controls, and benchmarking.

Information governance plays a key role in empowering organizations to comply in a cost-effective and efficient manner. It ensures smooth operations, proper delegation of authority, and the management of risk. Governance helps to overcome the inertia of "silos"—organizational, functional, and process silos—and reduce the challenge of tracking, monitoring, and reporting on regulations. To minimize error and control costs, organizations need to have a framework in place to help manage these processes and controls and inform all employees about the necessity of implementing governance while meeting reporting and auditing demands.

Security and Privacy

There is a systematic correlation between investing in compliance and enforcing information security. In many sectors, the ever-present threat of security breaches is driving investments in information governance. In 2020, with increased access to personal information, the digital enterprise will be required to ensure information systems are protected and individual rights are respected.

Many government policies are focused around national security and privacy. In the U.S., these regulations include the USA PATRIOT Act, the Homeland Security Act, and the Health Insurance Portability & Accountability Act (HIPAA). Canada's counterpart is the Personal Information Protection and Electronic Documents Act (PIPEDA). European equivalents include the Data Protection Act (U.K.), the EU E-Privacy Directive, and the Data Protection Directive.

As transactions and interactions become more digitally based, organizations will have to meter collecting volumes of personal data with protecting the privacy of this information. The mining of personal data is already a highly charged issue. In 2006, *Wired Magazine* blew the whistle on AT&T and Verizon for giving the National Security Council (NSC) access to network traffic without a warrant.[15] Google's 2012 privacy modification that permits the company to share data across services and third-party websites is fueling concerns about the storage of millions of user-based Internet searches and information in a cloud-based data warehouse.[16]

What would prevent these organizations from sharing information like this with any party, including the government? This is disconcerting at best. Google is the world's largest search engine, one of the top three email providers, a social network, and owner of the Blogger® platform and the world's largest video site, YouTube. Facebook has the social contacts, messages, wall posts, and photos of more than 750 million people.[17] At the moment, private sector policies on data protection and law enforcement are not consistent or clearly articulated across borders and organizations.

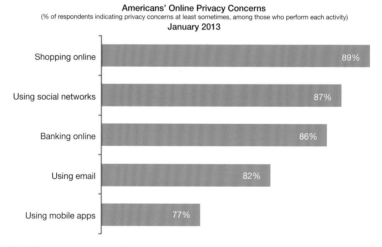

Americans' Online Privacy Concerns
(% of respondents indicating privacy concerns at least sometimes, among those who perform each activity)
January 2013

Shopping online — 89%
Using social networks — 87%
Banking online — 86%
Using email — 82%
Using mobile apps — 77%

FIGURE 7.6: Roughly 9 in 10 Adults in the U.S. Worry About Their Online Privacy[18]

[15] Ryan Singel, *"Whistle-Blower Outs NSA Spy Room"*, Wired Magazine, July 2006, http://www.wired.com/science/discoveries/ news/2006/04/70619 (accessed February 2014).

[16] Bob Brown, *"Google previews new privacy policy"*, Network World, January 31, 2012, http://www.networkworld.com/ news/2012/013112-google-privacy-policy-255529.html (accessed February 2014).

[17] James Ball, *"Me and my data: how much do the internet giants really know?"* The Guardian, April 22, 2012, http://www.theguardian.com/technology/2012/apr/22/me-and-my-data-internet-giants (accessed July 2014).

[18] Derickson, *"Americans' Online Privacy Concerns"*, e-Strategy Trends, January 29, 2013, http://trends.e-strategyblog.com/2013/01/29/americans-online-privacy-concerns/7737 (accessed July 2014).

The USA PATRIOT Act, created to prevent terrorism post-9/11, gives the U.S. government broad powers to access personal data. With provisions extended by the President, the PATRIOT Act has become a trade issue in selling cloud computing services due to fears that providers could be forced to hand over data to U.S. authorities. This means essentially that any company that deals with a company in the U.S. can have its records accessed by the U.S. government. Fears about security of information caused governments in Europe to consider banning U.S.-based cloud firms from competing for government contracts.[19] So who owns information in the cloud and who protects the data? And, in the wake of big data—with many different data points amassed, examined, compared, and analyzed—how will this impact privacy for the 2020 consumer?

Casting Digital Shadows

In 2020, the digital enterprise will collect information from the digital shadows cast by its customers. Online interactions and devices will be tracked to determine the sum total of data shared online. Algorithms will be used to predict customer preferences, interests, purchases, and more. There are already services available today that trace digital shadows, such as myshadow.org and Ubisoft's "Digital Shadow", which assigns a dollar value to an individual's personal data.

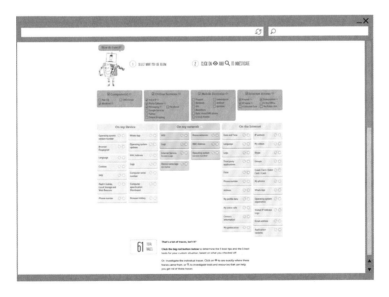

FIGURE 7.7: Tracing A Digital Shadow[20]

---

[19] David Saleh Rauf, "PATRIOT Act clouds picture for tech", Politico, November 2009, http://www.politico.com/news/stories/1111/69366.html (accessed February 2014).

[20] Trace My Shadow: *https://myshadow.org/trace-my-shadow* (accessed September 2014).

When consumers visit a website, often they are asked for a name and email address in order to access information. Some even ask for title, company, and profession. Stage two authentication requests a phone number to protect an account from being hacked. The value of social media exponentially increases based on the amount of information its subscribers enter. Facebook tracks likes, comments, pictures and videos shared, groups joined, and events attended. All of this data is highly accessible to host sites that can make it available to third-party organizations—and it is free.

In 2020, personal data may not be free as consumers barter to exchange their personal information for goods and services. A technically savvy consumer will demand quality engagement or goods and services in exchange for their personal data. Society will have to determine the cumulative value of personal data.

In the future, both public and private sector organizations will have to manage information effectively and transparently to ensure the accuracy and authenticity of sensitive data. Large-scale data mining will be strongly regulated. Record-keeping processes will be streamlined on a common information management infrastructure to simplify and secure the processing of information. As society becomes digital and the Internet engenders a faster pace of crime, governments and regulators will need to focus on the development and enforcement of interoperable policies, standards, and systems to prevent identity theft and online fraud.

Where Do Security Threats Come From?

As digital technologies have evolved, so have information security threats. Attacks today are multi-stage, hard to discover, and highly targeted. From organized crime syndicates to hacktivists, vulnerabilities permeate all levels of enterprise IT systems.

In 2013, more than two million stolen passwords used for sites such as Facebook, Google, Yahoo®, and other web services were posted online.[21] Login data was taken from computers that were infected with malicious software. The stolen information could be used to extract and then sell people's personal information. In February of the same year, Microsoft® announced that it had been hacked following a series of cyber-attacks.[22]

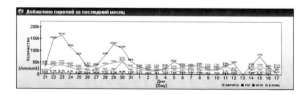

FIGURE 7.8: Malware Scraped Details from Users on a Daily Basis[23]

[21] BBC News, *"Stolen Facebook and Yahoo passwords dumped online"*, December 4, 2013, *http://www.bbc.co.uk/news/technology-25213846* (accessed January 2014).

[22] Damon Poeter, *"Microsoft Joins Ranks of the Tragically Hacked"*, PC Magazine, February 22, 2013.

[23] BBC News, *"Stolen Facebook and Yahoo passwords dumped online"*, December 4, 2013, *http://www.bbc.co.uk/news/technology-25213846* (accessed January 2014).

The costs associated with data breaches are staggering. In 2012, losses related to identity theft totaled $21 billion in the U.S. alone. The average annualized cost of cyber breaches for 56 benchmarked organizations was $89 billion. The largest insurance claim payout was $20 million, and overall, there was an 18 percent increase in average financial losses associated with security incidents from 2012 to 2013.[24]

Companies and their data are vulnerable. In 2020, cyber security will be a critical requirement for combatting trends such as nation-state backed espionage, more vulnerable service providers, big data, mobile apps, encryption failures—all exacerbated by an IT skills gap. Even today, the value of information must be considered in the context of security. The protection of corporate Intellectual Property (IP) is becoming an increasing concern for IT organizations as confidential information is housed in digital format. Threats from both inside and outside the company must be considered.

While many organizations have good external defenses in place, the real threat of a security breach comes from unauthorized access by employees. As was the case with the WikiLeaks incident and the National Security Agency-PRISM scandal, the risk of security breach is often from the inside out. The rise of the mobile workforce contributes to this, increasing risk through the lack of clearly defined or implemented BYOD policies, instances of lost or stolen devices, or the accidental sharing of confidential information across devices.

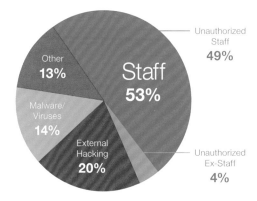

FIGURE 7.9: The Most Likely Source of a Security Breach[25]

[24] "Threat Horizon 2016", Information Security Forum (ISF), 2014.

[25] Mark J. Barrenechea and Tom Jenkins, "e-Government or Out of Government", OpenText, 2014.

Another security-related consideration is the need to ensure disaster recovery. While it is a regular function of IT organizations to consider backup and recovery, this type of project highlights the importance of information and systems that are critical in protecting the enterprise from information loss.

When information needs to be retained for litigation or compliance purposes, the information must remain intact, defensible, and discoverable. Without the requisite controls and discovery mechanisms, information can become a threat to the enterprise. It could be the defense of a lawsuit or audit or the data required for submission to bring a new drug to market—in either case, compromising the information represents a financial and/or competitive risk to the enterprise.

Effective Risk Management

No real risk can be mitigated to a zero percent likelihood of occurring, and some risks are 100 percent likely to happen. So how can the digital enterprise determine which risks to mitigate and which consequences to prepare for? A risk profile helps the enterprise examine the likelihood of identified risks and their potential impact.

If an organization is a litigation target, it makes very little sense to try and prevent court action. Defensible deletion is a better tactic as it leads to reductions in discovery costs and legal fees. According to research, the average organization needs to keep one percent of its information for legal holds, five percent to meet regulatory requirements, and 25 percent for business analysis and insights. By implication, this research indicates that it is possible that 69 percent of enterprise information could be thrown out, without suffering negative consequences.[26]

Keeping everything means higher storage and infrastructure costs. It increases the cost of investigation as content must be searched, examined, and reviewed from all of its sources. With the dramatic growth in content volume, this approach becomes less and less tenable. The route to avoiding this is defensible deletion—when content is governed, understood, classified, and then managed consistently. An added benefit of a defensible deletion program is that it makes organizations more efficient by reducing the amount of irrelevant information that users have to sift through to get work done.

---

[26] Lorrie Luellig, *"A Modern Governance Strategy for Data Disposal"*, CIO Insight, *http://www.cioinsight.com/it-management/inside-the-c-suite/amodern-governance-strategy-for-data-disposal.html/* (accessed July 2013).

FIGURE 7.10: Policies and Controls Mitigate Risk

When creating a risk profile, it's important to look at the organization as a whole and assess the different types of information individually. Not all information is created equally and not all information exposes an organization to the same risk. Identifying information that is critical to continued business operations allows organizations to craft policies that result in expending resources where it provides the biggest benefit. Identifying information that, if lost or disclosed, would cause nothing more than a minor nuisance prevents organizations from expending resources where there is little appreciable gain. In other words, there's no point in buying flood insurance if your house is on a desert mountaintop.

The protection of enterprise information should be holistic, covering all bases to avoid information risks that might violate legislation, cause non-compliance, or adversely impact the organization's ability to perform. Digital governance allows access to information on a "need to know" basis, while preserving an overall integrated archive of information.

In the following feature, security and governance are top priorities for Bruce Power. CIO Sarah Shortreed discusses the challenges around protecting sensitive data in an enterprise IT environment.

Bruce Power

Bruce Power is Canada's first private nuclear generator. Its 2,300-acre site on the shores of Lake Huron is home to eight CANDU® reactors, each one capable of generating enough low-cost, reliable, safe, and clean electricity to meet the annual needs of a city the size of Hamilton, Ontario. Bruce Power has approximately 4,200 employees and is the world's largest nuclear facility, generating 6,300 megawatts to deliver power to over one in four hospitals, homes, schools, and businesses in Ontario.

Formed in 2001, Bruce Power is a partnership between TransCanada, Borealis Infrastructure Management, the Power Workers' Union, and the Society of Energy Professionals. A majority of Bruce Power's employees are also owners in the business. As a private entity, driving a profitable business for shareholders and stakeholders is top of mind for CIO Sarah Shortreed. In an asset-intensive and highly-regulated industry, Sarah's focus is on maximizing the life expectancy of the plant's critical assets—securely and efficiently—based on the convergence of IT and OT (operational technologies). Her strategy combines technology and operations, with a philosophy rooted in effective information management as the foundation for innovation and growth. What follows are excerpts from an interview with Ms. Shortreed.

FIGURE 7.11: Bruce Power

"Security is paramount. In a sector that's governed by longevity and security, we have to be selective about our investment in digital technologies. The nuclear industry is based on stability. We have just restarted two units that will now run for another 40 years. Some of these new, disruptive IT technologies have a lifespan of just three to five years. We need to think long term, so some are not a good fit. Within the plant, we have equipment and instruments that talk to each other to keep operations running smoothly. In the future we'll be securely connecting more sensors between machines and using automated systems to facilitate preventative maintenance, for example.

Our top information security challenges are information breaches, which compromise intellectual capital and proprietary information, as well as the cyber incidents that can affect our key systems. Like every business out there, we fight the day-to-day battles of viruses and phishing. Since many breaches in any company are often 'from the inside out' and assisted by unwitting victims, we are expanding our training program to encourage 'digital health' at home as well as in the workplace. It's a whole-life experience approach that's similar to health and wellness: if an employee's home life is more secure, then they'll bring that mentality with them when they come into work.

All of the information related to our core business must be managed to ensure security and compliance. The important thing for us is the life of the reactors and the plants. We're obligated by law and regulation to keep some records for the lifetime of the plant. Our retention schedules are for 'as long as the facility functions'. A drawing from 1965 has to be accessible and readable today. And a drawing that's drawn tomorrow will have to be accessible and readable 100 years from now. It's our job to ensure that records are preserved, protected, and accessible. For this reason, content management is one of our top critical infrastructure applications.

Having an information management system also helps us learn from our records. We have large construction projects with billion-dollar budgets. We need to be able to comb through project records and find the lessons learned, so that these can be applied to the next project. Our project-related information has to be consolidated and metadata applied so that once the project is complete, it can be accessed and used productively in the future.

As far as other disruptive technologies are concerned, we're using cloud, mobile devices, and communities of practice. On the non-core side of the business, we are moving non-operational systems, like human resources and finance, to the cloud. Since these systems don't contain nuclear data, having them in the cloud doesn't compromise our security. In this industry, for innovation to happen, there has to be a secure infrastructure in place. First and foremost information has to be secured and to standard. So there is a correlation between innovation and information. For example, CANDU® reactors are unique Canadian products and our engineers need access to accurate data, when and where they need it. That empowers them to make great engineering decisions.

We are also working to empower our employees using mobile devices. We're testing tablets in the field. Our plants are massive spaces—equivalent to the size of many football fields. A pilot mobile app helps field workers connect to critical information when they perform maintenance, for example. With a mobile device they can get all the information they want, when and how they want it. They can download specs, instructions, checklists, without leaving the worksite, which saves time, and reduces the chance of error.

Mobile apps will also appeal to our demographic, as 35 percent of our employees are under the age of 35. We want to channel the energy and fresh ideas these younger employees will bring with them to the plant, so we'll have to equip them with the tools they like to work with, like social and mobile technologies. But we're also thinking long term and building a legacy. People will work their entire careers in this industry. It requires a unique skill set. And again, that's where the platform is so important. We have to set up reliable IT platforms so that when someone wants to make a decision, they can find and access the content they need quickly— whether its Business Intelligence (BI), content storage, or risk management tools. If all those technologies are in place in a secure platform, then the immediacy the younger generations require will be there. This takes planning now to anticipate what parts of the platform will be important years down the road. For our industry, information management will always be a fundamental part of this platform.

A Holistic Approach to Governance

When an information governance system is implemented across the enterprise, the technology archives and manages content across all environments. Archiving ensures that content is stored only once and is accessible in the event of discovery or audit, reducing the time it takes to find information from weeks to mere hours. Storage and infrastructure savings can be multiplied with each content source that is brought under digital governance.

When an electronic investigation (audit or legal review) is initiated, these systems have to be examined, information identified, and policies well understood and documented. If policy is maintained centrally, then one central source can be understood, documented, and defended. This approach results in significantly less cost and time invested, instead of examining each and every different system of record for corporate information.

When organizations have disparate systems and no overall governance, content deletion becomes very difficult and ineffective. Before content can be deleted, it must be well understood and the corporate value of it assessed. A high percentage of organizations are not able to do this because they do not have complete governance—including content lifecycle management—in place.

Enterprise Information Management (EIM) delivers a seamless compliance, governance, and risk management solution. It connects procedural guidelines with documentation, process execution tools, reporting and audits, with Enterprise Resource Planning (ERP) systems. It brings consistency and scale to the management and preservation of information by incorporating records management with solutions for archiving, email management, search, and e-discovery.

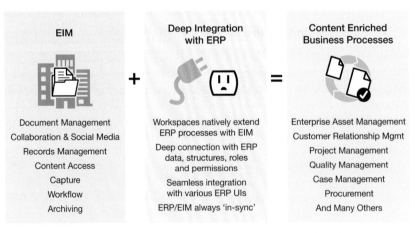

FIGURE 7.12: EIM - A Fully Integrated GRC Management Solution

EIM gives organizations the ability to apply governance across departments, content, and application silos. EIM manages the lifecycle of enterprise content, while embedding information directly into processes to give content a consistent context. Effective records management allows content like emails, documents, and paper files to be classified as business records and managed to comply with information governance and regulatory requirements. Combining structured and unstructured data to align with operations adds value to mainstream organizational activities.

Digital Governance Challenges

While governance is a growing priority for executives, many organizations do not believe they have reached a significant level of data governance maturity. "In fact, only 15 percent rate their data governance maturity as high or very high—defined as incorporating both business and IT, with top-level support and spanning major parts of the organization."[27]

Some organizations have implemented digital governance programs, faced governance challenges and been unsuccessful. This may be because they've not achieved strong enough user acceptance of the systems. Governance should be built into systems and processes rather than presented as a manual task for end users. The key is bringing the governance technology to the user's environment of choice and making it easy, enabling them to spend their time doing their daily activities instead of finding ways to get around using the system.

In addition to poor user adoption, governance challenges emerge when commitment from all governance stakeholders is not incorporated into digital governance planning from the outset. Members of the legal and compliance groups, IT, and line-of-business executives should come together to plan and implement an information governance program. Many organizations form a stewardship committee to make critical decisions about the program. Carefully choosing the members of the committee ensures commitment and decision-making power.

For most organizations, implementing a digital governance program is hindered by poor information management. Along with disparate silos, systems, and processes, information is further fragmented by the disruptive technologies that introduce new formats to the enterprise.

---

[27] Michele Goetz and Henry Peyret, et al., *"Data Governance Equals Business Opportunity. No, Really"*, Forrester Research, *http://www.forrester.com/Data+Governance+Equals+Business+Opportunity+No+Really/fulltext/-/E-RES83342* (accessed 20 May 2013).

Disruptive Technologies and Governance

Digital governance challenges are likely to increase in the short term. As connectivity becomes zero distance and devices are more powerful, the digital enterprise will be expected to control the flow of information in any format across every channel—from mobile devices and tablets to social media shared in the cloud. Challenges around compliance and governance will increase as digital content grows and people continue to use mobile devices and social software to create and share information. In the public domain, there are obvious data and privacy protection issues, along with security breaches and potential for reputation damage. How do government regulations such as HIPAA, PIPEDA, and the Stored Wire and Electronic Communications Act impact social media? Is it realistic for organizations to enforce corporate policy outside the work environment?

In 2020, the digital workplace will support a social, mobile workforce. Generation Z will work where and how they want to. Many will use mobile devices and social applications to create and collaborate on their content, resulting in corporate information existing outside the firewall, and more importantly, outside information governance policies. In the extended digital enterprise, end-to-end supply chain management will involve partners synchronizing data and collaborating outside the firewall. In many cases this will occur via cloud-based platforms and mobile devices.

As mobile devices are adopted by the enterprise, security will be a growing concern. Security on a mobile device is a combination of security over-the-air, over-the-wire, and permission-based access to systems. Mobile platforms can verify permissions much in the same way a web browser checks access permissions to an EIM repository or intranet. As data is transmitted or collaborative spaces accessed, the platform ensures that version history, audit capabilities, reports, security, and permissions contained with the system translate directly to the mobile device. Device governance is provided so that content can be stored and used on mobile devices, and if the device is lost, the content can be removed remotely.

Like mobile devices, social media introduces similar concerns around information governance and security. According to research, 58 percent of organizations today use social media to connect with their customers; in 2020, this percentage will be significantly higher.[28] Currently, social media is used without governance systems in place. Social compliance programs can help ensure governance and protect brand reputation. Organizations with social compliance programs in place are 15 percent less likely to violate requirements governing brands and organizational activities, avoiding costly impacts on brand image and legal repercussions. A social compliance program requires storing and centralizing social content in a secure EIM repository where it can be managed as a corporate record.[29]

[28] *"Social Compliance: Protect Brand Equity and Ensure Governance"*, Aberdeen Group, January 2012.
[29] Ibid.

As outsourcing to the cloud continues, and Software-as-a-Services (SaaS) becomes the standard platform for enterprise applications, organizations will be required to manage records in many locations. EIM provides visibility for IT governance and data management and reduces risk by eliminating duplication and supporting automatic disposition of records according to corporate policy. While mobile devices, social media, and cloud computing are paving the way for new opportunities and dramatic increases in productivity, widespread usage must be protected with the robust security and privacy mechanisms inherent in an EIM system.

Balance Matters

As the technology that underpins information governance, EIM is designed to protect information where it is used: at the point of interaction in the application itself, offering security mechanisms such as access and permissions, information audit capabilities, and secure information exchange built right into the system.

EIM will help the digital enterprise to create and maintain a trusted governance repository, through establishing controls that address information policies, procedures, business rules, and roles and responsibilities. Internal controls are typically based on processes designed to provide reasonable assurance regarding the effectiveness and efficiency of operations, reliability of financial reporting, and compliance with applicable laws and regulations.

FIGURE 7.13: Internal Process Controls

Once guidelines around GRC have been communicated, an organization needs to give employees the support they require to implement the defined processes. As a key component of EIM, Business Process Management (BPM) delivers an effective process control engine—initiating processes, defining and distributing tasks, recording their completion, and reporting on the outcomes of a given process. A governance system with a supporting best practices repository not only helps to support compliance and governance, it enables best practices to be followed and documented.

Digital governance is not just about complying with regulations and minimizing risk, it's about maximizing the value of the information to create a good, profitable business. It applies to all enterprise information, regardless of format, function, or location. Digital governance doesn't impede the enterprise's ability to do good business—it enhances it. It helps the enterprise to maintain stakeholder trust, improve transparency into performance and practices, reduce costs related to storage and e-discovery, and uncover new opportunities for business.

EIM provides an integrated GRC platform and all of the technology and services required to provide end-to-end digital governance. To thrive in a digital-first world, the strategic CIO must steward the digital enterprise to meet ongoing compliance regulations and requirements, identify gaps, and properly protect information to minimize risk and maximize value. In the following chapter, we examine the evolving role of the strategic CIO in more detail—and how EIM helps the CIO manage risk without curtailing the potential rewards of enterprise information.

CHAPTER **8**

THE STRATEGIC CIO

CHAPTER 8

The Strategic CIO

"Savvy CIOs will get their CEOs to recognize that changes being brought about by disruptive shifts come at an accelerated pace and a global level of impact. IT is no longer just about the IT function. Instead, IT has become the catalyst for the next phase of innovation in personal and competitive business ecosystems."[1]

In 2020, the enterprise will either evolve or it will become obsolete. As outlined in this book, a digital-first world will force a radical overhaul of enterprise strategies, processes, products, services, and relationships. To empower the digital enterprise, the strategic CIO will need to break out of operations mode to better align themselves with the business, embrace future trends in technology, and identify new value streams. Successful IT leaders of the future will apply the technologies described throughout this book to re-engineer and digitize old business models.

Technology is now a part of every aspect of business. As the structure of business changes in 2020, the IT functions and systems that support it will need to change as well—from software to processes to governance and the required skill sets. As innovators continue to disrupt industries, CIOs will have to restructure IT to accommodate the rapid pace of change. The IT organization will play a pivotal strategic role in digital transformation. This transformation will require a pervasive shift throughout the enterprise toward digitized tools, processes, and information that create customer value and competitive advantage. Managing and harnessing information is essential to driving digital strategies for innovation and growth.

In the year 2020, the attention of the strategic CIO will shift to systems of engagement to sustain strategies for growth and innovation. Over the last 30 years, CIOs have been focused on automating processes and transactions in systems of record with Enterprise Resource Planning (ERP) systems. For the next 30 years, CIOs will concentrate on automating processes and transactions for unstructured information in systems of engagement with Enterprise Information Management (EIM).

---

[1] Daryl C. Plummer et al, *"Gartner Top Predictions 2014: Plan for a Disruptive, but Constructive Future"*, Gartner Inc., October 7, 2013.

CIOs Are Under Siege

As emerging digital technologies promise to transform the way businesses interact with their employees, customers, and suppliers, CIOs need to understand both the threats and opportunities that disruptive technologies pose. For many organizations, however, digital disruption is poorly understood. While 74 percent of companies participating in a recent report have a digital strategy in place, only one-third of executives feel that their strategy is accurate, only 21 percent are confident that the right leaders are in place to guide and implement the strategy, and fewer still feel they have the skills and competencies needed to execute on a digital strategy. The responsibility falls on the CIO's shoulders to lead the discourse on digital transformation.[2]

The role of the CIO is transforming to accommodate many factors in today's global economy. The velocity of business is intense. For many companies (77 percent), more than one-third of their business processes rely on digital technology. As technology becomes the foundation for business, it can no longer be separated from the processes that it drives. As a result, the CIO must shift from tactical to strategic—from leading a reactive department that responds to requests to leading a department that proactively applies technology to enhance the business and anticipates how to support digital transformation.

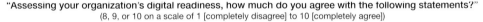

"Assessing your organization's digital readiness, how much do you agree with the following statements?"
(8, 9, or 10 on a scale of 1 [completely disagree] to 10 [completely agree])

Our CEO sets a clear vision for digital in our business — 21%

We have the right people to define our digital strategy — 21%

We have the necessary technology to execute our digital strategy — 19%

We have the necessary people and skills to execute our digital strategy — 15%

We have the necessary processes to execute our digital strategy — 14%

Base: 1,254 executives in companies with 250 or more employees

FIGURE 8.1: Executives Doubt their Readiness to Execute on a Digital Strategy[3]

---

[2] Nigel Fenwick and Martin Gill, *"The Future of Business Is Digital"*, Forrester Research, March 10, 2014.

[3] Ibid.

In a complex business landscape, the role of IT is also evolving beyond a mandate to "keep the lights on". Board members and executives are looking for IT to contribute more than operational responsibility to the enterprise. According to a report by *The Economist*, C-level executives believe the IT function will undergo substantial transformation: 57 percent of the 536 C-Suite executives surveyed expect their IT function to change significantly over the next three years and 12 percent predict a "complete overhaul." At least 43 percent say their company will increasingly use IT as a commodity service that is bought as and when needed.[4] The traditional centralized IT function is under tremendous pressure to support disruptive technologies, such as cloud computing, the proliferation of consumer-focused mobile devices and applications, and big data analytics. Many IT leaders struggle with balancing a vision of how IT can add value to the enterprise with ongoing levels of service and support, risk management, and program delivery.

"What level of impact will digital have on the following functions in the next 24 months?"
(8, 9, or 10 on a scale of 1 [no impact at all] to 10 [huge impact])

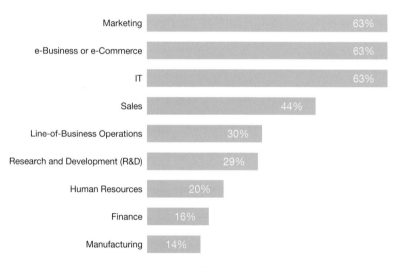

Base: 1,254 executives in companies with 250 or more employees

FIGURE 8.2: IT Is Being Digitally Disrupted[5]

[4] *"The C-suite Challenges IT: New Expectations for Business Value"*, Economist Intelligent Unit, The Economist, Jun 13, 2012, http://www.slideshare.net/Management-Thinking/the-csuite-challenges-it-new-expectations-for-business-value (accessed August 2014).

[5] Nigel Fenwick and Martin Gill, *"The Future of Business Is Digital"*, Forrester Research, March 10, 2014.

The same report found that two-thirds of CIOs feel their function is well aligned with the business, but less than one-half of C-level executives feel the same way about their CIOs. Only 46 percent of C-level executives say their CIOs understand the business and 44 percent say their CIOs only understand the technical risks involved in new ways of using IT.[6] Many CIOs are still perceived as enablers rather than strategic drivers of business. There is a gap between expectation and delivery: only 28 percent of CEOs characterize IT as offering proactive leadership, 34 percent describe the role of IT as poor, and 24 percent characterize IT as innovating only when pushed to do so.[7]

Both the CIO and the IT department need to change in fundamental ways. The strategic CIO will support sustainable business growth through infrastructure investments that increase the speed of business. In 2020, the strategic CIO will use technology to:

- Grow the business
- Create competitive advantage through differentiation
- Automate mundane processes
- Make better decisions
- Provide superior customer experience
- Engage with customers, suppliers, and employees in new ways

True transformation requires shifting mindsets around infrastructure, information, integration and innovation—all of which is possible when processes are based on accurate information.

Infrastructure

CIOs are continually faced with the complexity of many systems accumulated over the years. Legacy technology and a plethora of departmental, best-of-breed, and homegrown applications are crippling agility and innovation. Adding emerging technologies to the mix further complicates the IT landscape. Current CIOs and their IT departments are too often regarded by other business units as the "Department of No"[8], placing limits on business growth and development through protect-and-respond approaches to security. Instead, CIOs need to establish a holistic view of their enterprise IT foundation that is digitally based and structured to support agility and transformation. Efficiency and cost-savings can be realized through outsourcing to the cloud, virtualization, and data center optimization. As described in the previous chapter, governance, risk management, and compliance are key aspects of this integrated infrastructure.

---

[6] *"The C-suite Challenges IT: New Expectations for Business Value"*, Economist Intelligent Unit, The Economist, Jun 13, 2012, *http://www.slideshare.net/Management-Thinking/the-csuite-challenges-it-new-expectations-for-business-value* (accessed August 2014).

[7] Ibid.

[8] Gray, Patrick, *"The Department of No"*, TechRepublic, December 19, 2011, *http://www.techrepublic.com/blog/tech-decision-maker/the-department-of-no/* (accessed September 2014).

Integration

A holistic IT infrastructure requires integration of data repositories and enterprise applications. CIOs should strive for consolidation onto platforms that allow for rapid innovation and application development, based on continuous iteration and improvement. Many enterprise architectures are made up of unconsolidated data centers or siloed data repositories. Processes and information cannot flow freely across departments, efficiency is hampered, and data quality is low. Integration across silos and processes provides CIOs with the "glue" needed for end-to-end transparency across an extended enterprise of suppliers, partners, and customers. Integration enables access to big data to improve data quality, governance, and innovation.

Information

Many CIOS are not responsible for managing the information that their business depends on. Instead, their focus is on structured data management in ERP systems, with little understanding of the importance of unstructured information. As a result, IT manages more technology with more interfaces that their users are capable of adopting. The strategic CIO manages both structured and unstructured content and strives to provide business units with the technology tools they need, where they need them—from the desktop to mobile devices.

Innovation

CIOs will always be mandated to do more with less, but this doesn't necessitate a typical project-based and problem-focused approach that is constrained by Six Sigma® or ITIL® (Information Technology Infrastructure Library) frameworks. The strategic CIO implements solutions quickly, smartly, and sustainably. With a consolidated infrastructure in place, they can innovate to create processes, value, and experiences. Borrowing from an entrepreneur's mindset and a startup approach, their strategies are based on co-creation with vendors, suppliers, and customers.

2020 IT: The Way Forward

The 2020 strategic CIO will invest in disruptive technologies to empower their business. The enterprise infrastructure will be holistic and expansive to include the extended digital enterprise. The IT ecosystem will be consolidated and processes improved to support superior customer experiences and employee productivity. Under a strategic leader, IT will optimize access to technology across devices, applications, and systems. The CIO will also be responsible for driving the enterprise information strategy. Creative leadership and strategy will be the focus. Specifically, the strategic CIO will use technology to accomplish the following:

- Embrace digital disruption
- Align the business with technology through agile processes
- Implement systems of engagement
- Empower executives, users, customers, partners, and suppliers
- Focus on information as enabler

Embrace Digital Disruption

In 2020, a passive approach to disruptive technologies will lead to missed opportunities to create competitive advantage. CIOs who fail to evolve will lose their functions to other business teams, find themselves reporting to the CFO, CMO, or COO, and could even end up "on the chopping block". Strategic CIOs need to begin now to assess the potential of disruptive technologies for creating differentiation through next-generation business models, growing profit, and delivering money-saving market efficiencies.

Current IT spend is shifting. Although global investment in IT will be conservative (at 4.1 percent in 2014[9]), leading organizations place a greater importance on digital technologies like cloud computing, mobile, data analytics, and enterprise social networks. While certain technologies are seen as critical to business operations, a majority of organizations have identified e-commerce and data analytics (54 percent and 53 percent, respectively) as critical to their business in the coming years, especially with regards to increasing efficiency, improving customer experience, and attracting and retaining top talent.[10]

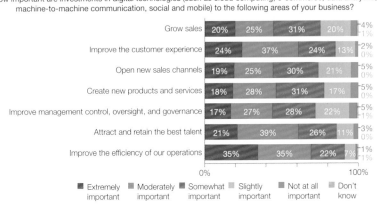

FIGURE 8.3: Importance of Investment in Digital Technologies[11]

[9] Marc Ferranti, "IDC cuts IT spending forecast on mobile slump, emerging market uncertainty", PCWorld, May 16, 2014, http://www.pcworld.com/article/2156520/idc-cuts-it-spending-forecast-on-mobile-slump-emerging-market-uncertainty.html (accessed August 2014).

[10] Sarah Murray, "CEO Briefing 2014 - The Global Agenda: Competing in a Digital World", Accenture, 2014.

[11] Ibid.

The same report finds that 70 percent of companies surveyed plan to use disruptive technologies like smart machines and automation to drive process efficiencies, while 45 percent will use them to find new revenue by expanding sales, opening new sales channels, or creating new products and services.[12]

In 2020, digital technologies like the Internet of Things (IoT), smart machines, digital printing, and wearable technologies will force organizations to explore new ways to engage with customers, create new products and services, and increase time to market. This moves beyond merely digitizing processes and, in many cases, will require radical shifts in core competencies, especially in IT. Smart machines, for example, will begin to infiltrate IT planning and infrastructure as automated replacements of human labor. CIOs will need to identify where these systems will improve efficiencies and reduce costs, how to implement them as standard equipment, additional benefits they may offer including increased safety, and changes in legislation, regulations, and liability that they might incur.

FIGURE 8.4: Increased Automation Through Robotics

The strategic CIO will need to position their IT organization in relation to these emerging digital technologies and build business use-case scenarios. This will entail monitoring advances in these technologies along with the information they produce in order to operationalize the technology. As mobile, smart devices, and analytics become ubiquitous, processes will have to change to support them. Technology will continue to force the enterprise to change business models quickly. In an intensely competitive landscape, the speed of business will shorten product lifecycles and call for faster times to innovate—and this will all be driven by technology.

---

[12] Sarah Murray, *"CEO Briefing 2014 - The Global Agenda: Competing in a Digital World"*, Accenture, 2014.

CIOs must be prepared to capitalize on the potential of information fueled by disruptive technologies, especially in terms of how they build apps to satisfy digital users and make their products, services, and infrastructure more flexible. As a smart Personal Assistant (PA), for example, Apple's Siri®, could serve as a "knowledge navigator" app that helps mobile users to find information or resources quickly and perform tasks based on web services that integrate with enterprise systems. As the lines blur between users and technology, the CIO will be responsible for exploring the cultural, ethical, and legal ramifications of deploying specific devices in an enterprise setting.

As disruptive technologies become part of the IT infrastructure, CIOs will grapple with information security as a growing challenge. Many organizations have experienced a cyber-security breach—more than 96 percent have experienced a significant IT security incident in the past year. While most admit to having inadequate security measures, only 33 percent are confident that they can improve these measures to prevent breaches in the future.[13] EIM systems are integral in preventing both internal and external data breaches.

Other challenges for integrating disruptive technologies into the enterprise architecture include the education, training, and skills needed to run these technologies. In a recent study, 42 percent of executives identified change management and 35 percent cited skills shortages as the biggest barriers to implementing digital technologies.[14] Overall, investments in digital technology are becoming a priority in many organizations with a recognized impact on enabling opportunity and innovation.

The strategic CIO must take initiative to capitalize on the potential that disruptive innovation presents to the enterprise. The widespread adoption of digital technologies is already forcing IT departments to evolve to accommodate complex systems. Those that don't embrace these innovations will lose out as laggards in a digital-first marketplace.

Align Business with Technology

The relationship between business and IT will undergo radical changes in 2020. As business applications are outsourced to the cloud and easier to manage, IT skills will become decentralized and incorporated into departments. This will fundamentally change the relationship between the business and IT groups. Digital technologies will drive these changes and the digitization of information-centric processes across the enterprise. Line-of-business leaders will become empowered to manage their own solutions. The strategic CIO will facilitate these changes by implementing strategies for digital process transformation.

---

[13] Colin Barker, *"CIOs must grasp emerging digital business technologies or face being marginalized"*, ZDNet, July 15, 2014, *http://www.zdnet.com/cios-must-grasp-emerging-digital-business-technologies-or-face-being-marginalised-7000031604/* (accessed August 2014).

[14] Murray, Sarah, *"CEO Briefing 2014 - The Global Agenda: Competing in a Digital World"*, Accenture, 2014.

To transform the enterprise to a digital enterprise, CIOs will need to broaden their role beyond the IT function to strategically align with other business executives. Expanding their role will require making changes to leadership skills, the IT organization, enterprise technologies and architecture, and IT skills and talent. Success will be based on effective collaboration with business units and executives to deliver on corporate goals and contribute directly to the success of the enterprise.

Corporate goals include improving time to market. In 2020, the strategic CIO will partner with the heads of Research and Development (R&D) and marketing to create an environment that fosters innovation across geographically distributed teams. Innovation begins with market research and discovery and is developed through collaborative ideation and rapid development processes to targeted demand creation. A partnership with marketing will facilitate objectives in terms of awareness, demand generation, and field enablement.

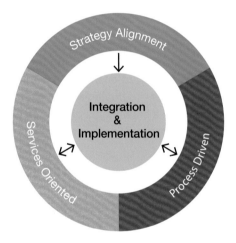

FIGURE 8.5: New Strategic Function of IT

Decreasing time to revenue is another important corporate goal that is particularly critical for product manufacturing functions such as operations, assembly, and production. The strategic CIO will partner with line-of-business managers to focus on operational excellence, quality, and cost by optimizing the supply chain and manufacturing processes using digital technologies.

Improving time to satisfaction requires the strategic CIO to partner with the heads of sales and services to deliver a seamless, engaging customer experience from awareness to purchase through to follow-on digital services. The goal is to transform customers into repeat buyers over an extended lifetime of value. As discussed in previous chapters, engagement is delivered through personalized, compelling, and consistent customer experience across all channels.

All of these corporate goals can be achieved through the implementation of an EIM strategy and supporting information and process management technologies. The decisive strength of EIM is its ability to cross departments, applications, and repositories to integrate with existing ERP systems across value chains and make information available for daily use. EIM embeds information management and security directly into processes, combining structured data with unstructured data to align operations with strategic vision. EIM arms executives with the technology and approaches they need to transform and empower the digital enterprise.

Implement Systems of Engagement

As the enterprise moves from governing systems of record to enabling new systems of engagement, the strategic CIO will help to articulate a digital strategy that balances innovation and growth with security and risk.

Enterprises are already evolving from systems of record to systems of engagement. Systems of record are the ERP systems that run an organization's business (financials, Customer Relationship Management (CRM), Human Resources (HR), etc.). As records, data has to be accurate, accessible, and integrated. Systems of engagement are systems that engage employees, such as email, social networks, collaborative technologies, and learning systems. Systems of engagement are digital and interactive, and will support the digital enterprise in 2020.

This shift is demonstrated by a change in focus from customer transactions to customer interactions; from hierarchical command-and-control systems of governance to flat, globally-enabled collaboration; and from facts and commitments to ideas and even nuances. With systems of engagement, discovery and dialogue influence the single source of the truth and conversations are communal, replacing documents as primary record types. Usability is intuitive, accessibility is *ad hoc* and open, and retention is transient. Finally, policy moves from concentrating on security mechanisms to protect corporate assets to protecting the privacy of enterprise users.

In 2020, the strategic CIO will build the digital enterprise according to a digital strategy that focuses on information as a key competitive differentiator in creating opportunity and mitigating risk.

Facilitate Agile Process Development

According to one report just 75 percent of IT budgets are dedicated to maintenance and updates[15], making it a challenge for IT to allocate resources and solutions to transform processes. Business leaders, however, will not wait for IT to implement solutions: they'll outsource these to the cloud, leaving IT behind while they pursue their own information and process management solutions.

---

[15] *"Why isn't IT spending creating more value?"*, PriceWaterhouseCoopers, June 2008.

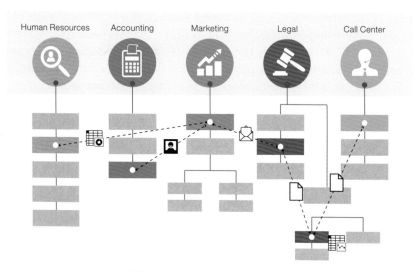

FIGURE 8.6: End-to-End Process Agility

In 2020, IT will have to adapt to support changing business models with new processes. Strategic CIOs will do this by transforming their systems of record into systems of engagement to support dynamic, mobile, and real-time customer transactions. This will fundamentally change business processes, which will have to move beyond departmental silos to support customer-centric processes. Agile process development and dynamic processes like case management will enable the digital enterprise to be more nimble and focused. Processes will move beyond packaged applications to EIM and Business Process Management (BPM) tools that are cross-functional, dynamic, easy to change, and repeatable.

Transformed processes build upon systems of record and integrate with customer-focused technologies using Smart Process Applications (SPAs). Future enterprise infrastructures will have to expand to support and incorporate the whole business ecosystem. Process integration will increase the speed of business. New processes will be deployed on premise, in the cloud, and to support mobile apps. CIOs will have to expand their function beyond the firewall to deliver value and business growth. Enterprise architecture will have to extend beyond the enterprise to incorporate new business models based on the needs of employees, customers, and partners and suppliers.

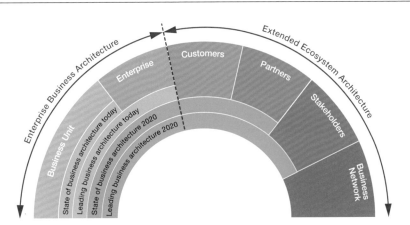

FIGURE 8.7: The Extended Enterprise

Business will be transformed through the consolidation of technology onto platforms that allow for rapid application development of next-generation products, replacing development that moves at the speed of "zero-fault" tolerance. Continuous iteration, rapid feature enhancement, and short-term solutions will be developed as cheap, fast, and scalable pilots, replacing longer deployment cycles and the IT backlog that hinders the ability to capitalize on new opportunities. In implementing these new applications, the strategic CIO will not be afraid to take risks or fail.

Empower the Digital Enterprise

In 2020, spending on cloud software, platform, and infrastructure services will grow from approximately $28 billion today to $258 billion in 2020—reaching 45 percent of total IT services spend.[16] As infrastructure moves to public or private clouds, the demand for IT to implement and maintain systems will be reduced. Software-as-a-Service (SaaS) will become the norm and IT will increasingly be seen as a "broker" of technologies, providing consulting services to employees and customers who are driving technology decisions. As services move to the cloud, IT will have more time and resources to focus on digitization and empowering end users through self-service applications and bring-your-own devices.

Agile and process-driven IT teams will replace the current structure of IT, no longer confined to organization around siloed technologies like servers, storage networks, desktops, mobile, and departmental systems. To add value to the enterprise, IT will have to shake off the shackles of legacy systems and their associated operating costs and inflexibilities and open up to the possibilities of co-creating or crowdsourcing solutions.

---

[16] Jean-Pierre Garbani, "Prepare For 2020: Transform Your IT Infrastructure And Operations Practice", Forrester Research, October 24, 2013.

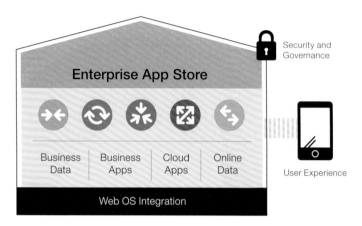

FIGURE 8.8: App Store Infrastructure

The trend toward the consumerization of IT will continue as individual users and consumers drive product and service design. The digital enterprise will focus on developing mission-critical apps and making these available from architecture that allows for the development of mobile apps and distribution in a private cloud. In essence, every agency that maintains a firewall and a proprietary repository of content could create a private cloud apps environment. Self-service kiosks provide a set of very personalized apps unique to each department or business unit. EIM makes this infrastructure possible by providing a set of integrated tools for managing process and information applications, while guaranteeing security and privacy.

Tech-savvy employees and customers will become self-sufficient. IT departments will struggle to control the corporate use of consumer-oriented technologies, but resisting this trend will impede digital transformation. In fact, 37 percent of U.S. information workers today use consumer technology to address business requirements, and more than half admit to having better technology at home.[17] IT will be required to match or exceed experience with consumer technologies like social networking and mobile apps. The strategic CIO will embrace the social revolution to move at the "speed of the customer."

Consumer-oriented technologies are far easier to access, use, and manage than many enterprise systems—giving employees the confidence they need to use mobile apps, social networks, and cloud computing to do their jobs. Employees are already circumventing IT to work more efficiently. In the digital enterprise, everyone will be an IT expert, to some degree, as technology becomes core to the business. Flexible IT portfolios will support the business using enterprise apps, BPM solutions, Dynamic Case Management (DCM), SPAs, social media, collaboration, and mobile apps.

[17] Tim Sheedy, *"The era of empowerment"*, CIO.com, December 23, 2010, *http://www.cio.com.au/article/370779/era_ empowerment/* (accessed August 2013).

The IT department will be required to optimize workforce experience through anytime, anyplace access to tools and information. They will need to accommodate demographics and a changing workforce with technologies that support the way they work. A good portion of the workforce will be remote: 66 percent of information workers in North America and Europe already work remotely.[18] IT will need to mobilize access to information and processes to accommodate these users.

In 2020, the IT landscape will become more multidimensional and complex—based on new business models, shifting corporate strategies, industry transformation, organizational changes, skill shortages, a multi-generational workforce, and digital disruption. To generate value for the business, CIOs will have to determine if current IT activities and projects contribute to the digital strategy and corporate objectives for growth. To master an infrastructure in flux, the strategic CIO will have to examine current processes, explore new business and engagement models, and embrace digital disruption—while maximizing security and minimizing risk. It's a tall order but with a sound EIM infrastructure in place, the strategic CIO is well equipped to digitally transform the enterprise.

Renew Focus on Information as Enabler

As part of consolidating the IT ecosystem and streamlining process integration, the strategic CIO stewards the enterprise information strategy. Well-managed information is central to increasing business growth, controlling cost, minimizing risk, and promoting innovation.

In 2020, the digital enterprise will leverage big data analytics to drive sales, performance, and opportunity.[19] The strategic CIO will invest in predictive and analytical technologies to deepen understanding into consumer preference, improve insights, and create more targeted offerings. The use of big data will accelerate in 2020. CIOs will add technologies to help them extract, analyze, and visualize complex data sets to the enterprise toolbox. Information gleaned will be incorporated into business processes and the insights used to drive more effective decision-making.

Recent research shows that the majority of CIOs believe that they are missing significant opportunities with their unstructured information. At the same time, they feel vulnerable to its risks. An EIM system empowers the enterprise to better understand its content, connect it to the right resources, and use it to innovate and find opportunity. To realize its true value, however, information must be managed and protected, especially in terms of privacy, security, and compliance. Despite having this knowledge, relatively few CIOs feel that they have a solid approach to EIM.[20]

[18] Connie Moore, "The Process-Driven Business Of 2020", Forrester Research, April 16, 2012.

[19] Garry Evans, "Disruptive Technologies: Winners and losers from game changing innovation", HSBC Global Research, October 2013.

[20] "Unleashing the Power of Information", CIO Magazine, 2012.

A strong EIM strategy is based on data integration across silos and systems, an increased access to accurate information, the standardization of customer information across the organization, improved information flow across processes, and data governance and security.

Disruptive innovation and advances in IT will empower employees, customers, partners, and suppliers through increased access to information. As discussed in this book, these stakeholder groups will drive new business models based on collaborative relationships across an extended digital enterprise. Information about products and services will become more accessible and create new levels of market transparency. To accelerate the pace of digital transformation, organizations need to ensure that information flows uninterrupted across functional silos and processes. EIM delivers a holistic approach to help ensure that information is accurate, integrated, and governed.

Beyond the enterprise, information can be opened up to create opportunity and drive economic development. Organizations in the public sector are opening up access to massive data sets to entrepreneurs to create products and services, develop targeted apps, and find new markets. The "Open Data" revolution—making information available in digital machine-readable format and reusable under open license terms—is well under way. Government is ahead of industry, but the digital enterprise will find value in opening up its information to allow external stakeholders to use information to create and crowdsource new products. Opening up the flow of ideas through external collaboration is a form of open innovation. For data to be shared, it must be managed and protected. EIM provides the balance between accessibility and security.

EIM combines systems of engagement with systems of record. Managing these systems of record—ERP systems that maintain finance, supply chain, resource planning, and human resources—will remain a critical function of the digital enterprise. The high-tech industry has spent considerable time and effort developing the solutions needed to support transaction-oriented processes that produce structured information. Part of the CIO's IT strategy will focus on consolidating these fundamental technologies. A good portion will be devoted to outsourcing to the cloud and orchestration. The strategic CIO will work with business leaders like the CMO to optimize customer engagement based superior customer interactions. EIM delivers the backbone required to streamline information-centric processes and securely support fully integrated customer experiences across many channels.

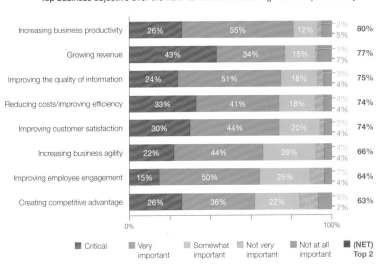

Top business objective over the next 12 months: Increasing business productivity

	Critical	Very important	Somewhat important	Not very important	Not at all important	(NET) Top 2
Increasing business productivity	26%	55%	12%	2%	5%	80%
Growing revenue	43%	34%	15%	1%	7%	77%
Improving the quality of information	24%	51%	18%	3%	4%	75%
Reducing costs/improving efficiency	33%	41%	18%	4%	4%	74%
Improving customer satisfaction	30%	44%	20%	2%	4%	74%
Increasing business agility	22%	44%	26%	4%	4%	66%
Improving employee engagement	15%	50%	25%	7%	4%	64%
Creating competitive advantage	26%	36%	22%	9%	7%	63%

FIGURE 8.9: Top Business Objectives Identified by Executives[21]

EIM helps to minimize and control risk. It protects Intellectual Property (IP) and enables CIOs to manage disruptions caused by a mobile workforce, unstructured data, the proliferation of devices, cloud computing, and social media. EIM systems can deliver benefits such as better data access and analysis, consolidation and standardization, reduced costs, and better alignment of IT activities with business objectives. But EIM does more than this—it provides a secure context in which innovation can happen. It unleashes the value of content, so that it can be discovered. Job #1 for the strategic CIOs is to establish clear EIM strategies and processes, which can then serve as a foundation to transformational business practices.

In the following feature, the Alberta Energy Regulator (AER) is applying disruptive technologies to information to streamline the regulatory process and empower both the organization specifically and the general public.

---

[21] *"Unleashing the Power of Information"*, CIO Magazine, 2012.

Alberta Energy Regulator

Energy regulation in Alberta spans more than 75 years and has evolved over time. In 2013, the Alberta Energy Regulator (AER) was established to regulate energy development in Alberta—from application and exploration to construction and development to abandonment, reclamation, and remediation. Today AER ensures the safe, efficient, orderly, and environmentally responsible development of hydrocarbon resources over their entire life cycle. This includes allocating and conserving water resources, managing public lands, and protecting the environment while providing economic benefits for all Albertans. The AER currently regulates over 181,300 wells and 415,000 km of pipelines, 782 gas processing plants, nine oil sands mines, more than 50 thermal *in situ* and 200 primary/enhanced schemes, 11 coal mines, and four coal processing plants.

Tara Mulrooney is Chief Technology Officer for the AER and is accountable for developing the technology strategy and services to support the business strategy. In the following excerpts from an interview with Mrs. Mulrooney, she discusses the roles that digital technology and information play in the transformation program at AER as they migrate to an integrated resource management framework.

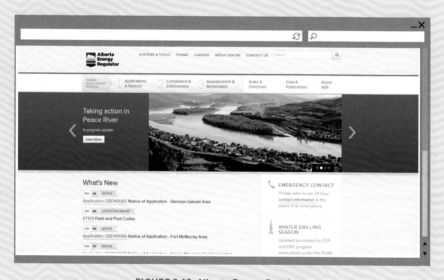

FIGURE 8.10: Alberta Energy Regulator

"We regulate the oil and gas industry for the province of Alberta. Very recently we took on new regulatory responsibilities to include jurisdiction for water, air, and biodiversity. We're the first of our kind and our mandate now includes the impact of development on the environment in terms of pollution, air quality, water usage, and increased engagement with our many stakeholders. With digital technologies making communications so far-reaching, social, and immediate, everything we do is under the microscope. Data and science are becoming more and more critical as we take on these additional responsibilities.

Digital technologies are having a profound effect on the oil and gas industries, especially in terms of collecting information on our projects for monitoring or compliance purposes. For example, remote sensors are now a part of every pipeline and every major project in the oil sands. They allow us to capture information in real time, so rather than requiring operators to physically report on compliance, we can access information and validate it ourselves. While this is a more efficient way of regulating compliance, it does present us with a big IT challenge because we have to be able to pull up information in our Geographic Information System (GIS)—a system that houses all types of spatial or geographical data—and correlate this data with sensor data.

When we start a project we need to be able to access any related information—whether its inspection reports, project plans, or surveys—for historical context. And it has to be integrated with the GIS and real-time sensor data. We have a wealth of information about every well that's ever been drilled in for Alberta for the last 75 years. With hundreds of thousands of oil and gas wells in Alberta, as well as oil sands and coal development, there is a lot of related infrastructure and many wells that are either producing or have stopped producing resources. Much of this information has been captured, stored, manipulated, analyzed, and managed as spatial or geographical data. When we hit thresholds on water, pollution, or noise, we need to refer to all of the unstructured content we have about a project. We're using digital technology to give our scientists and approvers instant, accurate, and integrated information at their fingertips in a single interface, and this is changing how we regulate today.

Right now our business processes aren't standardized, so regulation takes place on a case-by-case basis. Each project is affected by factors like geology, the risk to the operator, thresholds, and much of this changes hourly. We need tools like dynamic case management that allow us to route and change how we make decisions on the fly. As well as flexibility, we want a system that puts the business and workflow rules right in the hands of our users. If a scientist wants to do a cap rock integrity model they should just be able to route information to the field office and build this kind of application. It's a new way of looking at application development that could potentially wipe out ERP systems. ERP works great for commodity processes like finance or Human Resources (HR), but more and more businesses are fine-tuning their processes based on lightweight, flexible and personalized apps to become more agile and competitive. From a regulatory perspective, it gives us the ability to be proactive to any changes in regulations.

As part of our transformation program, we're working on using GIS to give organizations access to geological information, boundaries, roads, water bodies, and more so they can simulate the creation of a mine and receive the regulatory compliance rules that would be associated with the project. This new approach, based on improved access to information, helps increase efficiency and awareness about potential investment costs for example, around potential projects. The old approach was to model the data and focus on governance. These days, people are more technically savvy. They want immediate access to information so they can mash it up, apply it, analyze it, understand it, and present it in new ways. The younger generations especially don't understand the old world of SDLC (Software Development Life Cycle). Instead, they expect to be using tools and technologies that are bleeding edge, like Facebook and Google. We have to be aware of this in ways that we interact with stakeholders, engage the public, and communicate with our 1,200 employees located in 15 locations across the province.

We're also giving the public access to spatial information digitally. As Alberta grows and develops, we're seeing increasing construction in closer proximity to abandoned well sites or other energy infrastructure. We provide a website where people can go, click on a map of Alberta, zoom in, and find old well sites. We share this information with the Government of Alberta (GOA) and to date, it's the most publicly used interface at the GOA. A second project we developed is our new public notice of application tool. This was a key feature of our new regulatory mandate and required by legislation. The tool provides any Albertan who may have a concern with proposed activities in their area to learn more and formally express those concerns with the AER. Every time an application or approval goes through, it's published on our website within 30 minutes of the decision or application being made. The public can opt to submit a statement of concern which is reviewed as part of the application process. It's a great example of civic participation.

Our job is to educate and protect our users as they traverse the Internet. To do so, we need to make them aware of the risks and give them the tools they need to manage these risks. This involves a different security model. We are custodians of industry proprietary and trade secret data but we're trying to minimize collecting, managing, and storing so much information. Where possible, we're considering accessing information onsite with an operator, rather than storing it in a physical repository. In other words, do we need to keep all of the information we see? We are certainly concerned about all the typical phishing and hacking and from a generational perspective young people are pretty aware. The older generations need to be better educated because in the public domain people need to be cautious and accountable for the information they share.

As the younger generations enter the workforce, physical office space and standard hours will disappear. Work is more a part of people's lifestyles these days, and they want more flexibility with their work. Organizations that create an environment that empowers their people to work from any place at any time will be more successful. As we work more remotely, however, we'll need to find better ways to simulate face-to-face interaction and foster a sense of community. I think these are important aspects of communication. We have great communications tools with our smartphones and tablets, but we need a better way to meet and perhaps this will be achieved through teleconferencing or even holographic images.

The CIO Call to Action

"CIOs require a new agenda that incorporates hunting for new digital innovations and opportunities, and harvesting value from products, services, and operations."[22]

Given the benefits of deploying a comprehensive EIM solution and the risks of not doing so, in 2020, CIOs and other IT managers will make information management a top priority.

Digital executives have been able to bypass their technology colleagues in the past by turning to SaaS vendors or agencies. That approach isn't sustainable. Technology teams must step up, hire for digital skills, and help drive enterprise-wide transformation. This requires CIOs to champion a digital agenda by demonstrating how technology can facilitate change and making investments in EIM technology, systems, and processes to transform the business.

The journey to digital transformation requires a radical overhaul of culture, organizational structures, technology, and operating models. Since it is the new way forward, CIOs will need to figure out how to get there. EIM provides a strategic blueprint for transformational success. The next chapter outlines the key components and transformational benefits of EIM for the digital enterprise.

---

[22] Gartner, *"Gartner Executive Program Survey of More Than 2,000 CIOs Shows Digital Technologies Are Top Priorities in 2013"*, Gartner, Inc., January 16, 2013, *http://www.gartner.com/newsroom/id/2304615* (accessed March 2014).

THE DIGITAL ENTERPRISE

CHAPTER 9
The Digital Enterprise

"Enterprise Information Management (EIM) is the key transformative technology for the digital economy. It equips the digital enterprise with the ability to simplify, transform, and accelerate its business in a digital-first world."

We live in the time of unprecedented technologic disruption. Technologies ranging from mobile devices, analytics, and social media to cloud computing and the Internet of Things (IoT) are triggering innovations that are challenging the established rules of business. What all these technologies have in common is that they enable a new way of using information. Information is not just a cost factor—it has become the key to innovation, growth, and competitiveness. Information is becoming the core component of a corporate digital strategy.

We are entering the digital age, and information is becoming the currency of a digital economy. Information has replaced size, scale, access to resources, and geographic presence as a key driver of competitive advantage for the enterprise. Organizations that leverage their information to innovate and grow will be the ones that succeed.

In the digital-first world, digital information lies at the core of interactions, processes, transactions, and experiences. When information is harnessed and protected, the digital enterprise can reach the maximum level of efficiency, impact, and value while reducing security, compliance, and litigation risks.

Amidst these disruptions and the emergence of the digital economy, the goal for every organization is to transform itself to take full advantage of information and digital technologies—to become a digital enterprise to compete in a digital-first world. But how can the enterprise unlock the power of its information to transform itself, without compromising productivity and security? Enterprise Information Management (EIM) is the transformational technology that helps the digital enterprise innovate and thrive in a digital-first world. This chapter explores EIM as an integrated set of technologies and outlines an agenda for digital transformation.

EIM: A Platform for Transformation

A digital business, as outlined in Chapter 2, is one in which digital technology is both pervasive and central to its overall success. A digital enterprise, as we will describe further in this chapter, is a business that manages its information across its business ecosystem to drive value and competitive advantage. Digital enterprises adopt EIM as their foundational platform for change.

EIM is a set of technologies and practices that maximize the value of information as it flows across the enterprise. Its core technologies work together to create an end-to-end platform for sharing, collaboration, analysis, and decision-making, based on the effective management of information to harness its potential while mitigating risk through governance, compliance, and security.

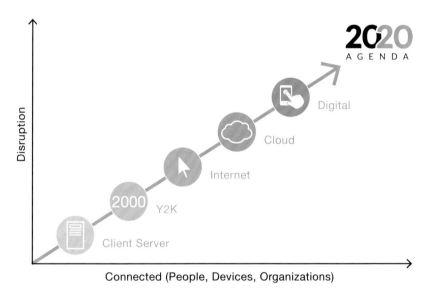

FIGURE 9.1: The Digital Enterprise - Re-Conceptualize the Future

An EIM framework supports the CIO to:

- Digitize all information assets and processes
- Build applications that drive the top-line results, such as revenue, customer satisfaction, innovation, and growth
- Integrate structured and unstructured data into a single source of the truth
- Facilitate social collaboration to foster engagement, idea sharing, and innovation
- Mobilize information and processes across any device, without compromising security
- Deliver a proven framework for information governance across all functions and applications
- Consolidate IT platforms and applications to manage information flows
- Protect the enterprise with robust, multi-layered security
- Capitalize on opportunity and expand into global markets

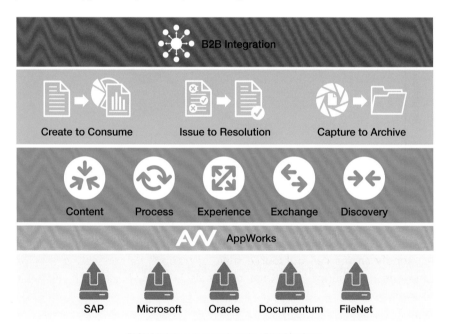

FIGURE 9.2: A Comprehensive EIM Platform

As depicted in the image above, EIM bundles core technologies together to add value as information flows across the digital enterprise. EIM is comprised of the following five integrated suites:

- **Process Suite:** Business Process Management (BPM) solutions for flexible, agile business processes that empower employees, customers, and partners to collaborate, streamline operations, and work efficiently.

- **Content Suite:** Enterprise Content Management (ECM) solutions for managing information throughout its lifecycle—from capture through to archiving and disposition—applying secure and consistent governance policies across any type of content.

- **Experience Suite:** Customer Experience Management (CEM) solutions for delivering responsive, compelling, and relevant user experiences across multiple channels to drive revenue, and customer satisfaction.

- **Exchange Suite:** Information Exchange (IX) solutions for exchanging complex or sensitive information quickly, securely, and reliably—between specific organizations or across a network of trading partners.

- **Discovery Suite:** Applications that derive value from growing volumes of content produced as the output of enterprise business processes or exchanged between business partners. These applications help the enterprise transition from query to insight to action.

In addition to the EIM suites, a development platform called AppWorks enables users to create purpose-built applications that assemble and consume enterprise information from across EIM suites in unique and highly customized ways.

Finally, Business-to-Business (B2B) integration technologies are used to manage information flows across an enterprise's entire business ecosystem. For instance, The Trading Grid is a cloud-based B2B integration platform that allows for the secure exchange of business documents with a global network of trading partners, quickly and efficiently. Also available as a fully managed B2B service, organizations with highly complex supply chains can outsource their operations by connecting with partners using multiple information exchange protocols in accordance with messaging and security standards.

This chapter describes each of the core EIM technologies and services in more detail. It includes stories about organizations that have embraced EIM to address the challenges of information and capitalize on its potential. Each story illustrates the transformative power of EIM.

Accelerating Processes with BPM

Business Process Management (BPM) is one of the core technologies of EIM. Whether conducting thousands of high-volume processes per day for case management or running a lower volume of high-value procedures, BPM helps organizations track the information that flows through their operations, gives them process knowledge, and enables them to optimize efficiencies.

Enterprise Resource Planning (ERP) systems lie at the core of business operations—managing everything from financials and human capital management to case management, vendor invoicing, and other critical aspects. Administrative work, like case management, forms the basis of many services or knowledge-based businesses. This type of work typically results in volumes of data housed in disparate databases across the business. Data generated by administrative activities is typically numerical and, in many instances, this information is not easily accessible. While ERP systems do an admirable job of executing process and serving as the system of record, they fall short when it comes to offering process agility and adaptability to changing business requirements.

As a result, BPM technology has moved beyond legacy processes and workflows to allow for the rapid modeling and automation of processes and the ability to easily update them. As illustrated in Figure 9.3, Smart Process Applications (SPAs) are evolving to support both structured and unstructured business processes and enable rapid adaptability to changing business requirements.

Business Process Integration	Business Rules Process Modeling Process Control	BPMS	BPMS +SOA	BPMS +MDD	BPMS +ACM	BPMS +Social	BPMS +Intelligence	Smart Process & Predictive/ Diagnostic Analytics
• Workflow • Enterprise Application Integration		• Web Services	• Mobile Driven Development • BPMN	Advanced Case Management (ACM)	Social Networks	Business Intelligence + Process Mining		
1990	1995	2000	2005	2009	2010	2011	2012	2013

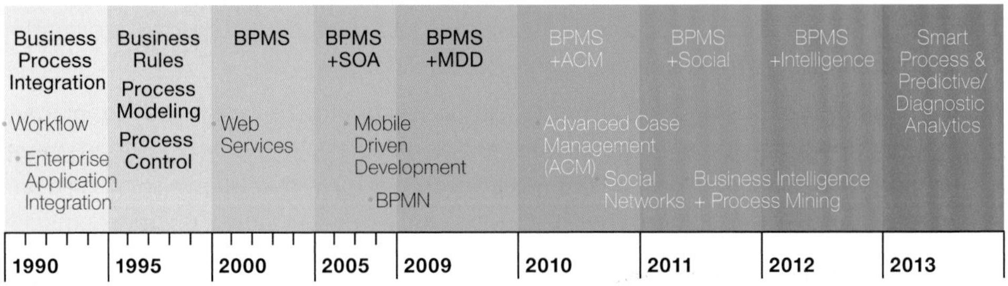

FIGURE 9.3: The Evolution of BPM

Digital Innovators: Federal Government Agency

In response to growing concerns about federal detention, a prominent G20 government established a federal agency to manage the confinement of persons in federal custody. With an average daily population in excess of 55,000 detainees across 94 federal judicial districts, they have an annual federal detention budget exceeding $1 billion. Operating under budget is a primary concern.

FIGURE 9.4: Business Process Management*

To reduce costs, the agency set about automating the administrative prisoner designation process—which crossed several independent organizations. The process of designating a convicted felon requires information contained in numerous documents and controlled by several agencies. In the past, each step of the process involved moving paperwork between multiple agencies and geographic locations using fax, postal mail, and FedEx®. The manual nature of this process led to slow processing times and limited audit trail capability with no way of effectively tracking status information.

The agency turned to BPM technology to streamline and digitize the designation process—while protecting sensitive prisoner information. Today, with access to a web server, all agencies can check on the status of any prisoners' designation document in real time. The solution provides easy access to all employees, regardless of location, and enables the agency to track, report on, and measure ongoing performance metrics. It is cost-effective, saves time, reduces errors, and provides transparency across the process. The system is currently operational in 82 districts and will be fully implemented in 94 judicial districts. Based on projected savings in the 82 districts, total approximated cost avoidance for all 94 districts would be $38.8 million.

---

* For demonstration purposes only. This is not an actual depiction of software running on the featured company's system.

Governing Information with ECM

As the governance facet of EIM, Enterprise Content Management (ECM) technologies are designed to help businesses manage an exploding volume of information and minimize the risks and costs associated with unmanaged content. Enterprise information is a critical asset in the digital business yet, as mentioned earlier, it carries risk if poorly managed. Access to increasing amounts of information requires a comprehensive ECM solution that can address demands for backups and auditing, tighter security, compliance, data classification (metadata), protection from threats of litigation, effective risk mitigation, and discovery technologies.

Content Lifecycle Management

End-to-end management as information flows through critical processes

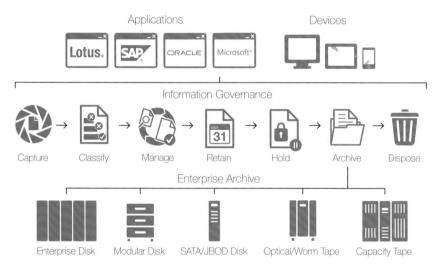

FIGURE 9.5: Managing the Full Lifecycle of Content

ECM provides end-to-end management of information as it flows through mission-critical processes throughout its lifecycle—from capture through to archive and disposition. It enables employees and business partners to share and collaborate on documents, control access to them, and manage versions efficiently. In addition, documents can be linked to a BPM workflow to ensure the latest version of content is used for business operations.

Many organizations look to their information systems to manage their business processes in the most efficient way possible and ensure competitive advantage through operational excellence and innovation. Virtually all business operations have content associated with them. Within business processes and applications, ECM plays an important role ensuring correct information is made available, actions on content are tracked and audited, and security is maintained.

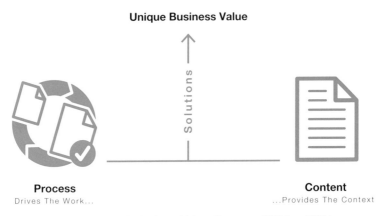

FIGURE 9.6: The Business Value of Integrated ECM and BPM

BPM combined with ECM drives timely decision-making and helps enforce compliance with corporate policy. The ability to create and work with business processes is built into ECM. Businesses build processes to review and approve document sets, create and manage procedures, manage projects and cases, and more.

Beyond process management, there are dedicated business applications built to address specific sets of business problems. Examples of these applications include Contracts Management, Regulated Documents, Invoice Management, Employee File Management, and Learning Management. The following story demonstrates how ECM makes content accessible and integrates critical content with business processes. ECM delivers a seamless experience across multiple environments, helping a world-class university unlock the potential of its information for greater access and innovation.

Digital Innovators: World-Class University

A large Asian university with more than 30,000 students and nearly 3,500 teaching and non-teaching staff offers over 230 programs on campus. The student population, number of employees, and courses offered have increased significantly over the years and led to a huge growth in data generated. With the intention to better manage and leverage this information, individual departments had implemented independent and isolated document management solutions. These disparate systems, however, were difficult to manage. Realizing that the ability to manage, control, and secure information was critical to their success, the university implemented ECM.

Managing information throughout its entire lifecycle creates business value and competitive advantage. From information capture to classification, management, storage, distribution, archiving, and disposition, ECM helps control the flow of information across various departments and administration within the university. Fast and seamless access from multiple environments (web, desktop, and mobile) within business processes and applications improves user productivity and organizational efficiency. The seamless integration of content with processes, collaboration tools, and social media platforms has addressed growing data needs, increased data integrity, and given the university better control over its content.

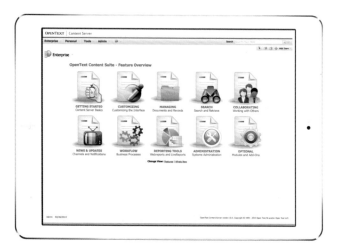

FIGURE 9.7: Enterprise Content Management[1]*

---

[1] Mark J. Barrenechea and Tom Jenkins, "e-Government or Out of Government", OpenText, 2014.
* For demonstration purposes only. This is not an actual depiction of software running on the featured company's system.

Delivering Exceptional Experiences with CEM

As one of the five foundational suites for EIM, Customer Experience Management (CEM) aims to create a richer, more interactive online experience—across multiple channels like websites, mobile devices, social networks, and more—without sacrificing requirements for information governance.

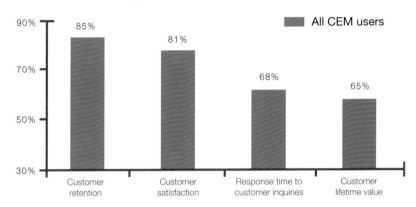

Percent of respondents indicating as valuable metrics to measure CEM performance, N=252

FIGURE 9.8: The Value of CEM

CEM powers the world's highest traffic brand sites, the most compelling mobile experiences, and the most recognized e-commerce portals on Earth. Managing the digital customer experience across multiple touchpoints in the journey, from reading a review or using a mobile app to conducting a transaction, a compelling experience is critical to success in the digital age.

As a comprehensive platform for managing media, web, social, and interactive content, CEM delivers a consistent user experience across multiple channels, while adhering to information governance policies and regulatory requirements. Media, website, and communications management capabilities combine to empower employees to optimize brand experiences. As described in the story below, a leading interactive entertainment agency uses CEM to manage its global brand.

Digital Innovators: Interactive Entertainment Agency

Global brand management is a key priority for a leading interactive entertainment agency. To optimize customer engagement, they strive to maintain a consistent look, feel, and voice across different regions and languages. Like many companies, their marketing content has traditionally been maintained in numerous systems, making it difficult to locate and distribute content, and ensure a consistent experience.

Using CEM, the agency established a centralized repository for their valuable digital content including broadcast commercials, print ads, and web content. For the company, the launch of a new title represents a significant investment and requires a highly coordinated, global team effort. With the system, internal users are now able to securely access these assets via the web as they develop new marketing campaigns. Once created, this marketing content is securely distributed to regional offices and affiliates across 26 territories and 8,500 employees throughout the world. Through this enhanced ability to reuse existing content, the company has increased its website traffic and revenue, while experiencing significant cost savings that are based on reductions in production and distribution costs.

FIGURE 9.9: Media Management[2]*

[2] Mark J. Barrenechea and Tom Jenkins, "e-Government or Out of Government", OpenText, 2014.

* For demonstration purposes only. This is not an actual depiction of software running on the featured company's system.

Secure Information Exchange

Information Exchange is the practice of conversational data exchange. It defines a set of offerings that support business conversations occurring internally among employees and externally with customers and partners—from electronic faxes and cloud services to large managed file transfers. These services generate truly massive amounts of data and are often tied into other practices, such as ECM, with very specific collection parameters.

As an EIM category of offerings, Information Exchange solutions help safely move information from where it is to where it needs to be, regardless of which business system it resides in, what devices it is required on and from user to user, company to customer— from anywhere at any time.

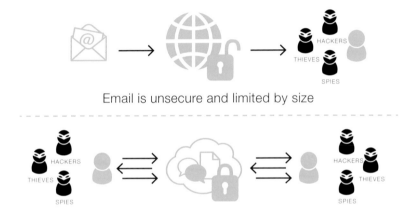

Email is unsecure and limited by size

Secure information exchange with messages, documents and extremely large files

FIGURE 9.10: Secure Information Exchange

Information Exchange empowers businesses to accelerate and control how information is delivered across the extended enterprise. Organizations can execute transactions in ways that are fast and secure. Data integrity and security are built in to protect against threats of internal information leaks and cyber attacks.

The opportunities to drive business value through effective, secure information exchange are countless and demonstrated in the story below about the cost savings realized by a company managing operations at a prominent international airport.

Digital Innovators: International Airport

One of India's busiest international airports is managed by a joint venture company that oversees its business operations. Each month, the company's employees send and receive hundreds of faxes to and from vendors and government agencies. Unfortunately, these paper-based methods were inefficient, and the close to 50 fax machines required consistent and costly maintenance. Along with the inefficiencies of handling paper-based faxes, there was a lack of security for sensitive documents sitting on fax machines.

With help from document delivery and fax software, the company has eliminated fax machine queues and gained reliable security for all faxed documents. Employees now send and receive documents without leaving their workstations. Instead of printing pages to feed through fax machines, employees can fax documents right from their desktop computers. Integration with email allows any sent or received fax to appear alongside emails for secure and easy reference, forwarding, or storage.

FIGURE 9.11: Secure and Streamlined Information Exchange*

Expenses associated with maintaining dozens of fax machines are now designated as cost savings. The company expects to eliminate close to 40 fax machines, keeping the remainder as backup devices in case of email failure. In addition to cost savings, new operational efficiencies are being realized. Faxes that used to take from 15 to 20 minutes to process are now delivered and tracked electronically within seconds. Employees who link to the office via mobile devices when they are traveling also stay on top of urgent faxes and staff members have increased efficiency because the solution has optimized their time.

---

* For demonstration purposes only. This is not an actual depiction of software running on the featured company's system.

Improving Insight and Reducing Risk With Discovery

As a facet of EIM, Discovery solutions organize and visualize all relevant information to make it possible to find and learn about the right information at the right time and place. The integrated set of technologies that comprise Discovery enhances an organization's capacity to "remember".

The expense and time associated with traditional legal or other information discovery is very high. Having a set of tools available to reduce the data sets retrieved in a discovery and make them more accurate represents immediate savings for an organization. Applying analytics to large data sets gives the digital enterprise insights into productivity gaps and can provide techniques for improving efficiency.

Discovery solutions leverage search, content analytics, and discovery capabilities. These solutions break down organizational information silos, integrate information from across the enterprise, and amplify the value of information through better access, collaboration, and content re-use. Business insight is gained by capturing, combining, and transforming information to identify relationships, risk, and new opportunities for growth. Improved transparency into outcomes allows for the consistent measurement and monitoring of performance metrics, arming businesses with the information they need to improve productivity and the quality of their performance. Unlocking this data or large data sets is critical to identifying new opportunities for growth, minimizing risk, and promoting innovation.

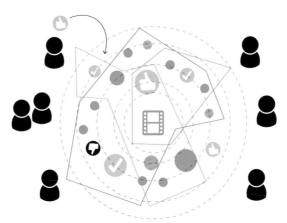

FIGURE 9.12: Semantic Pattern Recognition

With solutions like semantic search and content analytics, organizations like those in the feature below gain leading-edge capabilities to mine, extract, and present the true value of information for improved research and analysis.

Digital Innovators: Engineering Research Institution

One of the world's leading engineering research institutions makes major contributions to top national and international research via 9,000 employees and 24,000 students. According to its mission, the organization operates along three strategic fields of action: research, teaching, and innovation.

The institution needed a leading-edge solution that would give researchers, students, and the general public a faster way to find information across its 600 websites and the associated 200,000 web pages. On the back end, they required a robust website management solution that would support their 1,300 editors worldwide on a day-to-day basis by supplying metadata, key phrases, and the ability to automatically generate extracts of text—a collaborative platform that would bring together researchers, scientists, and students.

The institution implemented semantic navigation and content analytics in combination with website management to optimize web pages and provide relevant search results. Previously manual tasks that were labor intensive have been replaced by an automated solution that assigns metadata and supports entity extraction by generating teaser texts for new pages, saving users time and reducing error. Visitors are now given personalized access to highly relevant information facilitated by faceted search and related hits—resulting in a more satisfying end-user experience. With improved access to information and the ability to connect with researchers in similar areas of study, the website has evolved into an advanced research network that successfully meets the needs of all stakeholder groups.

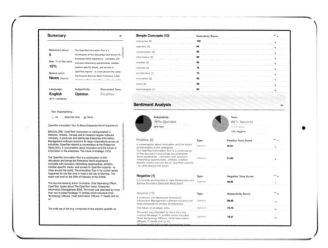

FIGURE 9.13: Content Analytics[3]*

[3] Mark J. Barrenechea and Tom Jenkins, "e-Government or Out of Government", OpenText, 2014.

* For demonstration purposes only. This is not an actual depiction of software running on the featured company's system.

AppWorks Development Platform

The digital enterprise is fueled by unrestricted access to information from within the enterprise and across the extended enterprise. AppWorks is an EIM technology designed to help streamline information flows across the digital enterprise. It is a common development platform that enables the creation of purpose-specific apps for information from any EIM core technology, making it available on a desktop, web interface, or mobile device. Examples of enterprise apps are depicted in Figure 9.14; development options are endless, limited only by business requirements and the imaginations of developers.

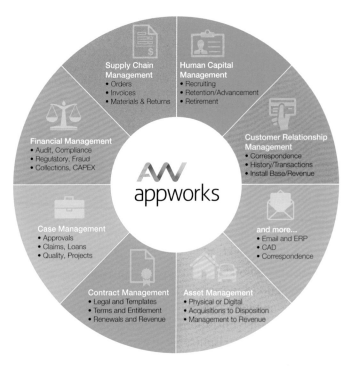

FIGURE 9.14: Building Enterprise Apps with AppWorks

Enterprise apps are built simply and easily using modern web technologies (HTML5, CSS3, and JavaScript), can be written once but deployed on any platform and can be managed securely from a centralized location. Using AppWorks, businesses can deliver push notifications to enterprise apps, deliver seamless application updates, collect usage reporting, and more. AppWorks makes it easy to manage and use enterprise information securely and conveniently in ways that accelerate innovation and drive business in the digital enterprise forward.

FIGURE 9.15: Fast, Simple Deployment of EIM Apps

Business-to-Business Integration

In a digital-first world, business operations rely on fast, efficient, and secure information exchange between employees and partners located around the world. Information Exchange is an important component of EIM for facilitating transactions and interactions within a global business network. B2B integration falls under the umbrella of Information Exchange solutions, yet focuses explicitly on managing information transmitted between supply chain trading partners.

B2B integration is a set of technologies that support the real-time, automated transfer of information, money, and goods and services, creating an "information supply chain" for the digital enterprise. It empowers a tightly integrated network of employees, suppliers, and partners to exchange communications, products, and commerce in ways that are rapid and accurate and to make decisions that are timely and intelligent.

Electronic Data Interchange (EDI) and integration services give organizations capacity for reliability and reach beyond traditional Value Added Networks (VANs). These technologies enable transactions while providing end-to-end visibility into supply chain operations for real-time decision making and improved orchestration of operations. As a result, efficiencies are increased as the number of items lost in transit is reduced, stock is proactively replenished, and equipment maintenance is scheduled for overall operational excellence.

The Trading Grid

The Trading Grid is a cloud-based B2B integration platform that enables the electronic exchange of business documents in a secure, fast, and reliable manner. Documents can be sent in XML and EDI document standards. The Trading Grid™ Messaging Service can be accessed via the Internet using a variety of communications options.

Managed Services

With supply chains becoming more complex, many organizations are outsourcing B2B integration to a third-party. Managed Services is a hosted B2B cloud service that provides the expertise, technical infrastructure, and process support for critical B2B programs. Managed Services experts perform all activities such as mapping, connectivity, onboarding, testing, monitoring, and end-user support to quickly connect business partners and resource projects on an as-needed basis.

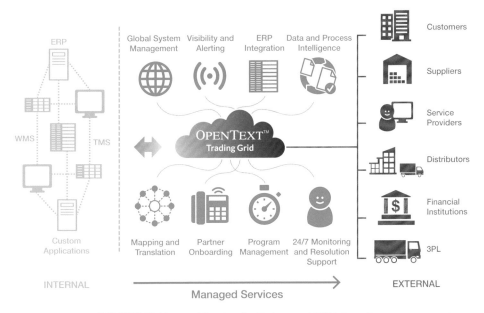

FIGURE 9.16: Managed Services for Outsourced B2B Integration

Digital Innovators: European Automotive OEM

A European automaker is one of the world's leading manufacturers of luxury, sports, and off-road vehicles. They have 25, 000 employees located around the world with manufacturing operations at multiple sites across the U.K. and India and a joint venture operation in China. They are a global organization with a complex supply chain.

When this company was divested from their parent company, they needed to establish their own B2B infrastructure while still maintaining continuity of operations and management of their global suppliers. They decided to focus on their core business competencies and outsource their entire B2B environment to B2B Managed Services.

The service team managed the onboarding of 1,000 EDI suppliers in North America and Europe and provided mediation between global standards. The platform was extended to support a new engine plant in the U.K. Today, the company has an efficient, tightly integrated global network of business partners, but the complexity of operating this network day-to-day is fully managed. The company has the option to integrate their B2B environment with their ERP system at a later date. As their operations expand over time, the company has the flexibility to scale their B2B network to facilitate growth.

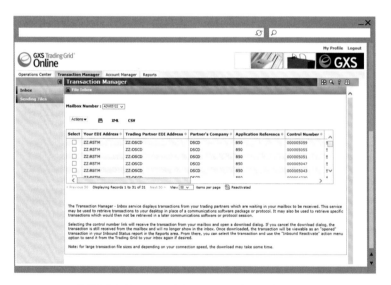

FIGURE 9.17: Managed Services Via the Trading Grid*

---

* For demonstration purposes only. This is not an actual depiction of software running on the featured company's system.

EIM: Bringing It All Together

The core sets of technologies and services described in this chapter form a comprehensive platform for EIM. As shown in Figure 9.18, an integrated EIM platform delivers better business results, improved relationships with customers, and helps to create an open, compliant IT infrastructure for business success in 2020 and beyond.

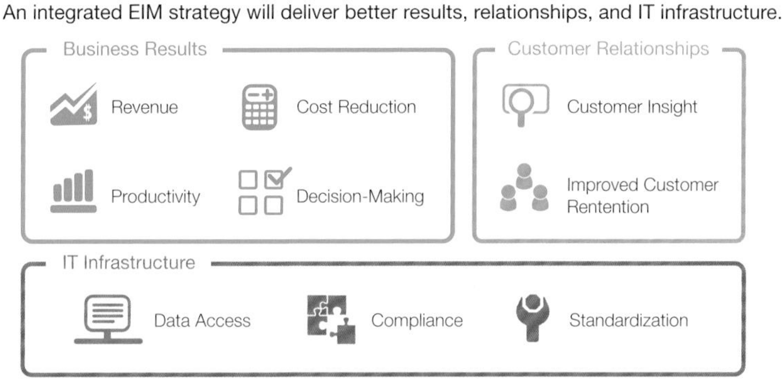

An integrated EIM strategy will deliver better results, relationships, and IT infrastructure.

Business Results
- Revenue
- Cost Reduction
- Productivity
- Decision-Making

Customer Relationships
- Customer Insight
- Improved Customer Rentention

IT Infrastructure
- Data Access
- Compliance
- Standardization

FIGURE 9.18: The Business Value of EIM

To become a digital enterprise, organizations must reduce cost, improve efficiencies, and increase their competitiveness by automating information processes. They must consolidate and upgrade their information management platforms for the requirements of a new workforce and new clientele in a new disruptive world. And organizations must increase the speed of information delivery through integrated systems within and beyond the boundaries of the enterprise. EIM helps the enterprise achieve all of the above, giving it the ability to simplify, transform, and accelerate its business in a digita-first world.

The priorities for change are clear: to effectively manage unstructured information and business processes; to automate B2B transactions that power business networks; to ensure security and privacy through information governance, compliance, and risk management; and to make access to information available from any application or device—on premise or in the cloud. By the year 2020, the most successful organizations will have already transformed themselves and the laggards will face unsustainable competitive pressure.

The time for change is now. As they start on a multi-year journey toward digital transformation, businesses are looking to IT for leadership. To help articulate this vision and execute on a plan for digital reinvention, the strategic CIO will partner with functional leaders across the enterprise. The following chapter explores change management strategies to help executives transform their organization into a digital enterprise to lead and succeed in a digital-first world.

STRATEGIES FOR
CHANGE MANAGEMENT

CHAPTER 10
Strategies for Change Management

"The biggest barrier to innovation in digital engagement is not technology but culture and lack of imagination."[1]

In 2020, success will depend on the enterprise's ability to transform itself into the digital enterprise. For transformation to be effective, the entire C-Suite—from CEOs to CMOs to CIOs—will have to articulate a vision of their organization as a digital enterprise.

To stay competitive, the enterprise must continually reinvent itself in a business landscape that is continually disrupted by technology. To maximize transformation, organizations need to create an environment in which innovation thrives. Business and technology leaders should be ready to take risks, follow digital strategies with effective leadership, and define new models of engagement. And they must be ready for a substantial shift in culture built on openness, innovation, and trust. Business problems should be examined and new processes created to solve them fearlessly and with imagination.

To make the digital vision a reality, IT will play a crucial role in supporting the enterprise's top business objectives. CIOs and other IT managers will need to highlight the connections between information management and core business objectives, and leverage technology to respond to the trends driving digital demand. In the future, transformational objectives will be rooted in Enterprise Information Management (EIM) strategies and solutions.

A holistic EIM solution is a fundamental enabler of digital transformation based on an integrated infrastructure that delivers secure information and services. An effective EIM strategy is guided by processes, principles, and standards.

Transformational Leadership

As explored in earlier chapters, CIOs and other leaders will have to develop the leadership capabilities required to drive digital transformation. To achieve digital advantage, business leaders will be called upon to motivate their companies around a strong, unifying vision articulated through an achievable and well-governed digital strategy. Typically, executives build their visions based on operational effectiveness (inside-out) or superior customer experiences and sales (outside-in). Centralization and digitization are fundamental to both approaches.[2]

---

[1] Malcolm Turnbull, *"Australian Minister Calls for Innovation in Digital Media"*, FutureGov Summit Australia, December 2013, *http://www.futuregov.asia/articles/2013/dec/04/australian-minister-calls-innovation-digital-gover/* (accessed February 2014).

[2] *"The Digital Advantage: How digital leaders outperform their peers in every industry"*, Gapgemini Consulting and the MIT Center for Digital Business, 2012.

The operations of any business could not be achieved without strong leadership based on a coherent strategy. A strategy accounts for cultural shift and technology infrastructure challenges while supporting engagement across departments, partners, suppliers, and customers. A transformational leader has to overcome outmoded structures and old management styles to empower Generation Z employees to self-direct, make decisions, experiment, generate ideas, and take risks. In 2020, the focus will be more on leadership than on management and designated "Information Czars" or leaders such as Chief Digital Officers may be appointed to lead the charge.

In order to build a digital business strategy based on disruption with EIM at its core, executives need to shift their focus away from cost efficiencies and tactical operations to providing value for the company through innovation, developing new products and services, and overall business growth. For the digital enterprise, the strategic CIO is often the champion of a strategy that is based on sound business practices enabled by technology.

CREATING A BUSINESS CASE

Transformational CIOs and business leaders need to establish a business case for digital transformation. What will the pay-back period be for the project? Most projects do not move forward without a scrutinized business case. A business case should be based on existing processes, industry best-practices, and the positive impact an EIM solution can have on performance.

Building Capacity

"Consumer data will be the biggest differentiator in the next two to three years. Whoever unlocks the reams of data and uses it strategically, will win."

- CEO OF BURBERRY, ANGELA AHRENDTS

As data has shown (see chapter 6), future spending will focus more on investments in human capital. The digital enterprise of the future will attract and build capacity by bringing together people with highly specific skill sets to collaborate on projects. To successfully transform, organizations will have to coordinate their initiatives and assign the right resources. More effective human capital management will be required, specifically by offering ways for employees to develop the skills required by future business models. Capacity can be built either by training existing employees or aggressively recruiting those with requisite skill sets. Organizations need to create and maintain a culture that both attracts and retains talent while supporting underlying values for diversity, corporate responsibility, and career development.

In 2020, for example, there will be an increasing demand for the skills needed to accurately analyze and extract insights from customer big data. As a result, entire departments could be designated to manage customer insights, requiring headcount and budget for customer data analysts. The digital enterprise will have to determine where its skills gaps lie, and either hire to fill these gaps or train and certify current staff to expand capabilities.

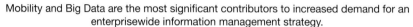

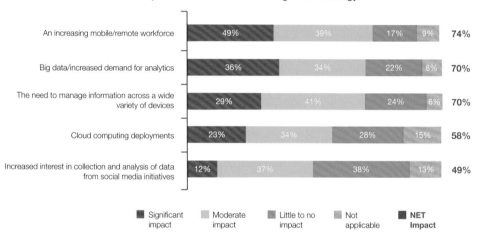

FIGURE 10.1: Near-Term Drivers for Technology Adoption Are Mobility and Big Data[3]

Building up communities of practice, promoting collaboration using corporate social networks, and allowing employees to bring their own devices into work and work remotely are ways of engendering a workplace that is attractive to an evolving workforce. Activities like innovation labs and highly focused "tiger teams" can be implemented and held accountable for producing actionable initiatives. In the customer-centric digital enterprise, individuals and teams can be rewarded for outstanding performance based on objectives linked to customer-focused initiatives to foster a sense of pride and ownership. Investment in digital education programs for executives helps to promote digital as core to overall growth and success—and aids in the trickledown effect in communicating the digital strategy as an enterprise-wide imperative. New team goals, performance plans, and incentives will have to be defined. The adoption of digital technologies will aid in building capacity. The 2020 workforce must be empowered to harness the potential of digital technologies and apply these to transform the business.

---

[3] *"Unleashing the Power of Information"*, CIO Magazine, 2012.

Redefining Processes

Moving away from traditional structures, practices, and solutions often requires starting from scratch in redefining processes. Effective technology leaders can add strategic value by driving the development of next-generation processes. In the digital enterprise, processes will be re-architected to support end-to-end customer-centric processes. EIM can be used to rapidly create new processes that support customer service—within hours—without requiring IT support or software development skills. By combining well-structured modules with pre-built components, an application-factory approach allows a line-of-business manager to build new processes easily. Alternately, an existing process can be used as a template and modified to suit business needs across customer service. This means that employees can be creative in anticipating service requirements and designing ways to address them. An on-demand environment is supported by flexible EIM infrastructure, new technologies, and the ability to re-engineer evolving customer processes and services.

New Models of Engagement

Collaborative EIM technologies facilitate the free flow of ideas and the exchange of knowledge. To truly transform, the digital enterprise will have to create networked environments based on new engagement models to empower all of its stakeholders in an extended enterprise. If employees are engaged, motivated, and unified under a consistent vision, they are less resistant to change. New engagement models often lead to a richer exchange of ideas, opportunities, and crowdsourced solutions. Inter-departmental collaboration helps to eliminate information and process silos.

Business units are more inclined to engage with IT to adopt new technologies and advance transformation. Externally, enterprise relationships are complex and difficult to manage, yet they offer a way to apply resources to projects that are beyond an organization's firewall, network, and scope. This dynamic requires a substantial shift in culture and good governance.

Redesigning the Supply Chain: B2B Integration

Business and technology leaders will have to work together in 2020 to integrate systems to support collaboration across value chains and the extended enterprise. From a change management perspective, many outmoded processes will be replaced with flexible and dynamic processes. The appropriate technologies will need to be in place to combine information and processes, based on cloud computing, mobility, data analytics and the Internet of Things (IoT). Old value chains will be replaced by responsive, resilient, innovative, and dynamic fulfillment networks. Connecting digitally to suppliers helps the enterprise more readily outsource specialized products or services.

Collaborative tools can be deployed for real-time and secure information exchange and the sharing of best practices between virtual, cross-functional teams. EIM provides a platform for this open market approach with visibility into supply chain logistics, streamlined information flows, and a secure single source of the truth across the digital enterprise. EIM helps to orchestrate logistics, increase speed of business, enable just-in-time delivery, and ultimately improve customer satisfaction. EIM is the glue that holds the extended enterprise together.

Enterprise Architecture

Enterprise architecture provides a framework for organizational change and includes plans for transitioning to future business models. Before resources are committed to implementing change, mapping and examining enterprise architecture can identify capability and risk. An enterprise architecture should outline ways in which data and information can be integrated with services effectively. Data integration—a critical enabling capability for transformation—must be reliable, secure, and accessible. Data integration combines operations and analytics to unify the enterprise. Enterprise architecture helps to ensure the interoperability of systems and the sharing of information resources across agencies. As an integrated suite of targeted functions, EIM supports digitization, data integration and discovery, customer experience management, secure information exchange, and records and information management.

Assessing (and Taking) Risks

Strong leadership directs transformation. To effect change, leaders should be willing to take risks and redefine processes. IT issues need to be addressed and a risk assessment completed. Where does the largest cost and risk exist? This is typically the starting point for many projects.

Leaders must continually quantify and monitor their progress toward digital transformation so that initiatives can be measured and refined. Key Performance Indicators (KPIs) and digital scorecards can be used to help measure impact and change corporate culture.[4]

How to create shifts in culture and support technology adoption are outlined in the feature below, an excerpt from an interview with ClearCadence, based on their experience with change management in government organizations.

---

[4] "The Digital Advantage: How digital leaders outperform their peers in every industry", Gapgemini Consulting and the MIT Center for Digital Business, 2012.

ClearCadence

ClearCadence provides their clients with innovative and cost-effective business solutions through the efficient deployment and integration of information technology. The Company partners with large federal, state, and local government agencies to re-evaluate, re-define, and improve their processes.

What follows is an excerpt from an interview with David Dye, Co-Founder of ClearCadence and Jim Conklin, Managing Partner of the BPM Division, ClearCadence.

FIGURE 10.2: ClearCadence

"Most of the projects span across agencies and touch multiple systems. A good example is a court system. The clerk's office is managing all the files, but the prosecution, the public defender, and law enforcement also need access to files. Coordinating multiple agencies is the bigger challenge, more so than the technology itself.

Moving from paper to electronic (often a first step) transforms the way they're doing business, so the adoption takes a generation phase. You have the younger people, and they adapt well because they have grown up using technology. But some of the older generation may be a bit fearful of technology and are uncertain about it. So the adoption levels are completely different. We build a process based on what the agency needs to move forward with. When it comes to some of the traditional judiciary structures, we manage change one-on-one when necessary.

Whether they're improving efficiencies, reducing cost, or adding durability to generate revenue—and the closer they can get their Return On Investment (ROI) model to align with a key performance indicator—that's what helps to justify the cost of the project. That gets an executive's attention. We typically ask our customers: 'What is the easiest project to implement that will provide the highest KPI?' An attainable first win that's realistic to achieve in allotted timeframes is critical.

The Court System in the U.S., for example, has experienced budget cuts, but they still have to produce with limited resources. We implemented a paperless project in one division of the court system. Court papers needed to be filed, put in a manila folder, and processed through the system. Content came in from various sources, including electronically through an e-filing solution. But these files needed to be verified with the clerk's office, processed for court review and/or signature, sent back to the clerk's office—all while keeping the attorney's office in the loop.

There is a lot of content flying back and forth across government organizations and locations. If I'm an attorney and I have an emergency case 30 miles away in a different building, when the process is digitized and automated, I can pull up the electronic file quickly and easily without disrupting my work. When the files are digitally stored, the government has an audit trail of everything. So it's much more efficient for all the agencies and the constituencies. The result is a combination of offering a better service level and doing so at a lower cost."

Challenges to Change Management

As a foundational aspect of any digital journey, adopting EIM poses technical, operational, and cultural hurdles. The challenges associated with implementing comprehensive EIM strategies are the lack of standard processes and designated roles and responsibilities for information management. Challenges beyond standardization are technical in nature and include the variety, velocity, and volume of information and the complexity of IT systems. Having information fragmented across silos also hampers effective management and poses potential risks.

The organizational and cultural obstacles to implementing EIM include making adjustments to behavior and adoption. Most organizations must make structural and chain-of-command decisions when they change their processes. In many highly regulated industries, for example, organizations have been working according to predictable, command-and-control structures and processes for years at the sacrifice of initiative and performance. The younger generations are more comfortable with the new ways of engaging and the adaptability required to respond to changing markets and consumer demands.

To further complicate change management, many organizations have multiple and uncoordinated information management efforts underway. In one study, respondents identified that only 15 percent of their current information management initiatives were highly integrated. The same study found that more than one-quarter of current initiatives were siloed and lacked cross-initiative coordination and common goals.[5] To combat this, CIOs need to establish a centralized EIM strategy and guidance to ensure discrete initiatives are prioritized, coordinated, and compatible.

Lack of standardized processes and/or organizational role definitions, as well as internal politics and cultural issues, are top barriers to implementing an enterprise-wide information management strategy.

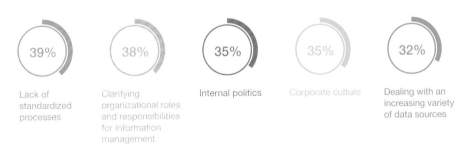

39%	38%	35%	35%	32%
Lack of standardized processes	Clarifying organizational roles and responsibilities for information management	Internal politics	Corporate culture	Dealing with an increasing variety of data sources

FIGURE 10.3: Challenges to Implementing an EIM Strategy[6]

---

[5] *"Unleashing the Power of Information"*, CIO Magazine, 2012.

[6] Ibid.

The risks of failing to establish a comprehensive EIM solution can be significant. These include decreased levels of productivity and performance, increased cost and IT burden, limited insight and poor decision-making, compromised security and the inability to comply with regulations.

Implementing an EIM Strategy

The benefits of deploying a comprehensive EIM solution are clear. Overall, EIM helps the digital enterprise align its efforts under a common vision and structure, engage all stakeholders, and govern their efforts. In 2020, CIOs and other IT managers will make EIM a top priority.

IT is no longer simply a provider of information. In 2020, IT will be responsible for empowering people with information that is usable. For this to happen, the digital enterprise needs to be able to access, manage, and protect its information—and make it actionable for a wide range of stakeholders.

When implementing an EIM strategy, a good first step is to take inventory of current enterprise information assets. This includes the following:

- Fragmentation - How many disconnected sources, flows, and archives do you have?
- Velocity - Which information processes are accelerating or need to do so?
- Variety - What kind of information, media, documents, and discussions are you most concerned with?
- Volume - How much information are you talking about?
- Security - What kind of information security risks are most threatening to your organization?
- Governance - How are you ensuring that your digital efforts are coordinated, efficient, and moving in the right direction?
- Compliance - Which legal or regulatory requirements and risks exist in your company and your industry?[7]

Efforts need to be prioritized and targeted—and linked to an articulated business case. Prioritization should align with the executive team's top business objectives, whether they are productivity, cost reduction, revenue growth, innovation, competitiveness, or governance. The objective that benefits most significantly from improved information management should be identified. These business needs are the pilot projects for effective digital transformation.

[7] *"Unleashing the Power of Information"*, CIO Magazine, 2012.

As EIM projects or initiatives are successful, they can be expanded to encompass more users, technologies, and processes. As discussed in Chapter 9, the core technologies of EIM include business process management, content management, customer experience, information exchange, and discovery. When these technologies are integrated, the full spectrum of transformational benefits can be realized, based on a data-driven approach.

Digital transformation is an ongoing process. Transformational leaders must be flexible and organizations agile enough to accept this truism. Beyond structural adjustments, a change of attitude is already underway. Many organizations are adopting entrepreneurial, innovative approaches to communicating and collaborating and taking steps to digitize their operations.

There are many examples of significant performance improvements. All of the stories and interviews included in this book are about digital transformation. The vision of transformation is being defined and recognized as one that will be in a perpetual state of flux. So structures and processes must subsume this, and journeys down the path to making the vision a reality will be many and variant. The good news is—as we have illustrated throughout this book—the technology is available, and many enterprises have already taken their first steps toward implementing a digital strategy with Enterprise Information Management at its foundation.

BIBLIOGRAPHY

Bibliography

Anderson, Chris. <u>Makers: The New Industrial Revolution</u>. Toronto, Canada: McClelland & Stewart, a Division of Random House Inc., 2012.

Anderson, Chris. <u>The Long Tail</u>. *http://www.longtail.com/about.html* (accessed May 2014).

Austin, Tom. *"Watchlist: Continuing Changes in the Nature of Work, 2010-2020"*. Gartner, Inc.: March 30, 2010.

Baker, Pam. *"BabyX Reads its First Words—Artificial Intelligence is Growing Up"*. FierceBigData: August 27, 2014. *http://www.fiercebigdata.com/story/babyx-reads-its-first-words-artificial-intelligence-growing/2014-08-27* (accessed Aug 2014).

Ball, James. *"Me and my data: how much do the internet giants really know?"* <u>The Guardian</u>: April 22, 2012. *http://www.theguardian.com/technology/2012/apr/22/me-and-my-data-internet-giants* (accessed July 2014).

Barker, Colin. *"CIOs must grasp emerging digital business technologies or face being marginalized"*. ZDNet: July 15, 2014. *http://www.zdnet.com/cios-must-grasp-emerging-digital-business-technologies-or-face-being-marginalised-7000031604/* (accessed August 2014).

Barrenechea, Mark J., and Tom Jenkins. <u>e-Government or Out of Government</u>. Canada: OpenText, 2014.

Barrenechea, Mark J., and Tom Jenkins. <u>Enterprise Information Management: The Next Generation of Enterprise Software</u>. Canada: OpenText, 2013.

Bartels, Andrew and Connie Moore, et al. *"Smart Process Applications Fill A Big Business Gap"*. Forrester Research: November 2012.

Bernstein, Paula. *"Did Netflix Really Put Blockbuster Out of Business?"* Indiewire: February 4, 2014. *http://www.indiewire.com/article/did-netflix-put-blockbuster-out-of-business-this-infographic-tells-the-real-story* (accessed September 2014).

Bersin, Josh. *"A New Organizational Learning Model: Learning On-Demand"*. Bersin by Deloitte: October 1, 2007. *http://joshbersin.com/2007/10/a-new-organizational-learning-model-learning-on-demand/* (accessed September 2014).

Bodine, Kerry, and Ron Rogowski. *"2013 Customer Experience Predictions"*. Forrester Research: January 3, 2013.

Bower, JL., and C. M. Christensen. *"Disruptive Technologies: Catching the Wave"*. <u>Harvard Business Review</u>. January-February 1995.

Brown, Bob. *"Google Previews New Privacy Policy"*. *http://www.networkworld.com/article/2185336/data-center/google-previews-new-privacy-policy.html* (accessed February 2014).

Burkett, Michael, Steven Steutermann, and Noha Tohamy. *"Digital Marketing, Internet of Things and 3D Printing are Digital-Business-Driven Disruptions for Supply Chains"*. Gartner, Inc.: March 11, 2014.

Burns, Rick. *"Study Shows Business Blogging Leads to 55% More Website Visitors"*. HubSpot. August 17, 2009. *http://blog.hubspot.com/blog/tabid/6307/bid/5014/Study-Shows-Business-Blogging-Leads-to-55-More-Website-Visitors.aspx* (accessed April 15, 2013).

"CEO Briefing 2014: The Global Agenda: Competing in a Digital World". Accenture: 2014. *http://www.accenture.com/SiteCollectionDocuments/PDF/Accenture-Global-Agenda-CEO-Briefing-2014-Competing-Digital-World.pdf* (accessed July, 2014).

"Cisco Consumer Experience Report for Automotive Industry: Survey of 1,511 Consumers in 10 Countries". Cisco: May 2013.

Colony, George F., and Peter Burris. *"Technology Management in the Age of the Customer"*. Forrester Research: October 10, 2013.

"ComScore". invodo.com. *http://www.invodo.com/resources/statistics/* (accessed March 2013).

"Customer Experience Management: Using the Power of Analytics to Optimize Customer Delight". Research Preview, Aberdeen Group. *http://www.brandchannel.com/images/papers/531_aberdeen_group_wp_customer_experience_management_0911.pdf* (accessed February 2013).

Davis, Diana. *"Case closed? The Difference Between Dynamic Case management (DCM) and Business Process Management (BPM)"*. Process Intelligence Network (PEX). *http://www.processexcellencenetwork.com/business-process-management-bpm/articles/case-closed-the-difference-between-dynamic-case-ma/* (accessed July 2014).

"Dubai Cops May Try Google Glass to Catch Speeders". rt.com: May 21, 2014. *http://rt.com/news/160552-dubai-cops-google-glass/* (accessed May 2014).

Duke, Peter. *"Sitting On Top of the World – A Strategy for Life (and Business)"*. Peter Duke Media Services: March 10, 2010. *http://dukemedia.com/sitting-on-top-of-the-world/* (accessed Sept 2014).

"Enterprise Governance, Risk and Compliance Market". MarketsandMarkets: 2014. *http://www.newportconsgroup.com/wp/wp-content/uploads/Brochure-Enterprise-Governance-Risk-and-Compliance-Market2013-2018-Primary.pdf* (accessed July 2014).

Erickson, David. *"Americans' Online Privacy Concerns, January 2013"*. e-Strategy Trends: January 29, 2013. *http://trends.e-strategyblog.com/2013/01/29/americans-online-privacy-concerns/7737* (accessed July 2014).

Essany, Michael. *"Major Mobile Trends Show Global Mobile Industry is now the Fastest Growing Market in the World"*. MobileMarketingWatch.com. July 7, 2011. http://www.mobilemarketingwatch.com/major-mobile-trends-show-global-mobile-industry-is-now-thefastest-growing-market-in-the-world-16840/ (accessed June 2013).

Evans, Garry. *"Disruptive Technologies: Winners and Losers from Game Changing Innovation"*. HSBC Global Research: October 2013.

Federico-O'Murchu, Linda. *"How 3D Printing Will Radically Change the World"*. CNBC: May 2014. *http://www.cnbc.com/id/101638702* (accessed May 2014).

Fenwick, Nigel, and Martin Gill. *"Digital Business Leadership"*. Forrester Research: December 18, 2013.

Fenwick, Nigel, and Martin Gill. *"The Future of Business Is Digital"*. Forrester Research: March 10, 2014.

Ferranti, Marc. *"IDC cuts IT Spending Forecast on Mobile Slump, Emerging Market Uncertainty"*. PCWorld: May 16, 2014. *http://www.pcworld.com/article/2156520/idc-cuts-it-spending-forecast-on-mobile-slump-emerging-market-uncertainty.html* (accessed August 2014).

Ferrari, Bob. *"GXS-The Hidden Gem in B2B Information Services and Application Support"*. The Ferrari Consulting and Research Group LLC *http://www.theferrarigroup.com/supply-chain-matters/2012/06/14/gxs-the-hidden-gem-in-b2b-information-services-and-application-support/* (accessed July 2012).

Friedman, Thomas L. *"Most Overblown Fears: Globalization"*. Newsweek: 2010. *http://2010.newsweek.com/top-10/most-overblown-fears/globalization.html* (accessed July 2014).

Gantz, John, and David Reinsel. *"The Digital Universe in 2020: Big Data, Bigger Digital Shadows, and Biggest Growth in the Far East"*. IDC: December, 2012.

Gantz, John. *"The Expanding Digital Universe"*. IDC: March 2007.

Garbani, Jean-Pierre, *"Prepare For 2020: Transform Your IT Infrastructure and Operations Practice"*. Forrester Research: October 24, 2013.

"Gartner Executive Program Survey of More Than 2,000 CIOs Shows Digital Technologies Are Top Priorities in 2013". Gartner, Inc.: January 16, 2013. *http://www.gartner.com/newsroom/id/2304615* (accessed March 2014).

"Gartner Reveals Top Predictions for IT Organisations and Users for 2013 and Beyond". Gartner, Inc.: October 24, 2012.

"Gartner Says the Internet of Things Installed Base Will Grow to 26 Billion Units By 2020". Gartner, Inc.: December 12, 2013.

"Gartner Top Predictions 2014: Plan for a Disruptive, but Constructive Future". Gartner, Inc.: October 7, 2013.

"Generation Z." Wikipedia. *http://en.wikipedia.org/wiki/Generation_Z* (accessed July, 2014).

Gens, Frank. *"IDC Predictions 2013: Competing on the 3rd Platform".* IDC: 2012. *http://www.idc.com/research/Predictions13/downloadable/238044.pdf* (accessed February 2014).

Ginovsky, John. *"Compliance Needs Tech Booster".* ABA Banking Journal: July 21, 2014. *http://www.ababj.com/blogs-3/making-sense-of-it-all/item/4774-compliance-needs-tech-booster* (accessed July 2014).

"Global Flows in a Digital Age: How Trade, Finance, People, and Data Connect the World Economy". McKinsey & Company: April 2014.

Goetz, Michele, and Henry Peyret, et al. *"Data Governance Equals Business Opportunity. No, Really".* Forrester Research. *http://www.forrester.com/Data+Governance+Equals+Business+Opportunity+No+Really/fulltext/-/E-RES83342* (accessed 20 May 2013).

Goetz, Michele, et al. *"Are Data Governance Tools Ready for Data Governance?"* Forrester Research: June 25, 2014. *http://blogs.forrester.com/michele_goetz* (accessed July 2014).

Gray, Patrick. *"The Department of No".* TechRepublic: December 19, 2011. *http://www.techrepublic.com/blog/tech-decision-maker/the-department-of-no/* (accessed September 2014).

Hall, Christopher. *"Digital Signage and the 'Store of the Future".* Retail Customer Experience: Dec 10, 2013. *http://www.retailcustomerexperience.com/articles/digital-signage-and-the-store-of-the-future/* (accessed July 2014).

Hammersley, Ben. Now For Then: How to Face the Digital Future Without Fear. London, UK: Hodder & Stoughton, 2012.

Heaney, Bob. *"Supply Chain Visibility. A Critical Strategy to Optimize Cost and Service".* Aberdeen Group: May 2013.

Heraghty, Mark. *"The Workplace of 2025 Will Be Wherever You Want It".* BBC News: September 2012. *http://www.bbc.com/news/business-19639048* (Accessed May 2014).

Herrera, Frederico. *"The Digital Workplace: Think, Share, Do".* Deloitte Canada: 2011.

Higginbottom, Karen. *"Managing Generation Z".* Institute of Leadership & Management: April 22, 2013. *https://www.i-l-m.com/Insight/Edge/2013/April/managing-generation-z* (accessed September 2014).

Horrigan, David, and Alan Pelz-Sharpe. *"451 Data: Information Governance Falls Flat Despite the Hype"*. 451 Research: February 20, 2014.

Howe, Jeff. *"Crowdsourcing: A Definition"*. Crowdsourcing: June 2, 2006. *http://crowdsourcing. typepad.com/cs/2006/06/crowdsourcing_a.html* (accessed February 2014).

"Infographic: 2013 Mobile Growth Statistics". Digital Buzz Blog: Oct 1, 2013. *http://www. digitalbuzzblog.com/infographic-2013-mobile-growth-statistics/* (accessed August 2014).

"Information Governance Reference Model (IGRM)". EDRM. *http://www.edrm.net/projects/igrm* (accessed July 2014).

Ingram, Katie. *"Change Your Marketing Approach for Generation Z"*. Forrester Research: February 19, 2013.

Ingram, Katie. *"US$83 Billion Lost Yearly in Marketing Due to Poor Customer Experience"*. CMSWire: May 29, 2013. *http://www.cmswire.com/cms/customer-experience/ibm-us83-billion-lost-yearly-in-marketing-due-to-poor-customer-experience-021084.php* (accessed June, 2014).

"Internet Use Reaches 5 Billion Worldwide". Future Timeline.net. *http://www.futuretimeline. net/21stcentury/2020.htm#internet-2020* (accessed March 2014).

Jenkins, Tom. Managing Content in the Cloud. Canada: OpenText, 2010.

Jerez, Sergio. *"Barcelona in the Pocket"*. City of Barcelona: PowerPoint® Presentation, June 2013.

Keifer, Steve. Herding Geese: The Story of the Information Supply Chain. Self-published, 2011.

King, Jeremy. *"Faster is Better: How We're Optimizing Walmart.com"*. The @WalmartLabs Blog: July 24, 2014. *http://www.walmartlabs.com/2013/07/24/faster-is-better-how-we-are-optimizing-walmart-com/* (accessed July 2014).

Lacobucci, Mike. *"Looking Ahead to Globalization 2020"*. MultiLingual Computing. *http:// www.moravia.com/files/download/Globalization2020_MultilingualComputing.pdf* (accessed July 2014).

Laney, Douglas, and Andrew White. *"Agenda Overview for Information Innovation and Governance, 2014"*. Gartner, Inc.: January 10, 2014.

Lanier, Jaron. Who Owns the Future?. New York: Simon & Schuster, 2013.

Luellig, Lorrie. *"A Modern Governance Strategy for Data Disposal"*. CIO Insight. *http://www. cioinsight.com/it-management/inside-the-c-suite/amodern-governance-strategy-for-data-disposal.html/* (accessed July 12, 2013).

Mahoney, John, and Mark Raskino. *"CIO New Year's Resolutions, 2014"*. Gartner, Inc.: December 30, 2013.

"MakerBot and Partners Are Leading the Charge to Crowd Source A MakerBot Desktop 3D Printer in Every School in America". BusinessWire: November 12, 2014. *http://www.marketwatch. com/story/makerbot-and-partners-are-leading-the-charge-to-crowd-source-a-makerbot-desktop-3d-printer-in-every-school-in-america-2013-11-12* (accessed July 2014).

"MakerBot's New 3D Printer: The Thing-O-Matic!" MakerBot: Saturday, September 25, 2010. *http://www.makerbot.com/blog/2010/09/25/announcing-makerbots-new-3d-printer-the-thing-o-matic/* (accessed September 2014).

Manyika, James, and Michael Chui, et al. *"Big Data: The Next Frontier for Innovation, Competition, and Productivity"*. McKinsey Global Institute, McKinsey & Company: June 2011.

Manyika, James, Michael Chui, et al. *"Open data: Unlocking Innovation and Performance with Liquid Information"*. McKinsey & Company: October, 2013.

Markovitch, Shahar, and Paul Willmott. *"Accelerating the Digitalization of Business Processes"*. McKinsey & Company: May 2014.

McAfee, Andrew, and Erik Brynjolfsson. *"Big Data: The Management Revolution"*. Harvard Business Review: 2012. *http://hbr.org/2012/10/big-data-the-management-revolution/ar/pr* (accessed November 5, 2012).

McAfee, Andrew. *"Enterprise 2.0 is Vital for Business"*. FT.com: December 9, 2009. *http://www. ft.com/cms/s/0/2c473802-e4c4-11de-96a2-00144feab49a.html#axzz375JRaIwe* (accessed July, 2014).

McQuivey, James. *"Digital Disruption: Unleashing the Next Wave of Innovation"*. Forrester Research, Inc.: 2013.

Meister, Jeanne C., and Karie Willyerd. The 2020 Workplace. Harper Collins: May 11, 2010.

Millar, Rich. *"How Many Data Centers? Emerson Says 500,000"*. December 14, 2011. *http:// www.datacenterknowledge.com/archives/2011/12/14/how-many-data-centers-emerson-says-500000/* (accessed May 2014).

"Millennials at Work Reshaping the Workplace". PriceWaterhouseCoopers: 2011. *http:// www.pwc.com/en_M1/m1/services/consulting/documents/millennials-at-work.pdf* (accessed July 2014).

Minkara, Omer, and Aly Pinder. *"Next-Generation Customer Experience Management"*. Aberdeen Group: 2013.

Moore, Connie. *"The Process-Driven Business of 2020"*. Forrester Research: April 16, 2012.

Moore, Geoffrey. *"Systems of Engagement and the Future of Enterprise IT: A Sea Change in Enterprise IT"*. AIIM: 2011.

Morley, Mark. *"How the 'Internet of Things' will Impact B2B and Global Supply Chains"*. Driving B2B Blog, Posted October 15, 2013. *http://www.gxsblogs.com/morleym/2013/10/how-the-internet-of-things-will-impact-b2b-and-global-supply-chains.html* (accessed August, 2014).

Murray, Sarah. *"CEO Briefing 2014 - The Global Agenda: Competing in a Digital World"*. Accenture: 2014.

O'Kane, Bill, and Andrew White, et al. *"Predicts 2012: Information Governance and MDM Programs Gain Traction"*. Gartner, Inc. *http://www.gartner.com/id=1856616* (accessed July 2013).

Olavsrud, Thor. *"CIOs Need to Evolve or Be Left in the Dust"*. CIO Magazine. Jun 22, 2012.

Orlov, Laurie, et al. *"Closing the CEO-CIO Gap"*. Forrester Research: February 2007.

Pallozzi, Daniel. *"Predictions for Retail 2020: A New Brick and Mortar Experience"*. December 4, 2013. *http://www.thoughtworks.com/insights/blog/predictions-retail-2020-new-brick-and-mortar-experience* (accessed July 2014).

"Perspectives on Digital Business". McKinsey & Company: January 2012.

Plummer, Daryl C., et al. *"Gartner Top Predictions 2014: Plan for a Disruptive, but Constructive Future"*. Gartner, Inc.: October 7, 2013.

Poeter, Damon. *"Microsoft Joins Ranks of the Tragically Hacked"*. PC Magazine: February 22, 2013.

Powers, Stephen, and John R. Rymer. *"Unify the Digital Experience Across Touchpoints"*. Forrester Research: August 22, 2012.

"Prepare for 2020: Transform Your IT Infrastructure and Operations Practice". Forrester Research: 2012.

Ramos, Laura. *"Make B2B Marketing Thrive in the Age of the Customer"*. Forrester Research: May 21, 2013.

Rasmus, Daniel W. *"Global Trend 6: Fostering a Global Workforce in Dynamic Times"*. Ernst & Young. *http://www.ey.com/GL/en/Issues/Business-environment/Business-redefined---Global-trend-6--Fostering-a-global-workforce-in-dynamic-times* (accessed July 2014).

Rauf, David Saleh. *"PATRIOT Act Clouds Picture for Tech"*. Politico: November 29, 2011. *http://www.politico.com/news/stories/1111/69366.html* (accessed February 2014).

Rifkin, Jeremy. The Zero Marginal Cost Society. Palgrave Macmillan Trade: April 1, 2014.

Robinson, Adam. *"The Rise of Distributed Manufacturing and 7 Advantages over Traditional Manufacturing"*. Cerasis Blog: April 2, 2014. *http://cerasis.com/2014/04/02/distributed-manufacturing/* (accessed July 2014).

Rogowski, Ron. *"Digital Customer Experience Trends to Watch, 2013"*. Forrester Research: 2013.

Rogowski, Ron. *"The Unified Customer Experience Imperative"*. Forrester Research: May 7, 2013.

Scaduto, Michael. *"Make Way for Generation Z"*. In Context Magazine: December 9, 2013. *http://www.incontextmag.com/articles/2013/make-way-for-generation-z.html* (accessed July 2014).

Schmidt, Eric, and Jaren Cohen. The New Digital Age: Transforming Nations, Businesses, and our Lives. Toronto, Canada: Random House of Canada Limited Inc., 2013.

Sharma, Chetan.*"2013 Mobile Industry Predictions Survey"*. Chetan Sharma Consulting: January 2013. *http://www.chetansharma.com/MobilePredictions2013.htm* (accessed May 2013).

Sheedy, Tim. *"The Era of Empowerment"*. CIO.com: December 23, 2010. *http://www.cio.com.au/article/370779/era_empowerment/* (accessed August 2013).

Shehadi, Ramez T., et al. *"Designing the Digital Workplace: Connectivity, Communication, Collaboration"*. PriceWaterhouseCoopers: 2013.

Singel, Ryan. *"Whistle-Blower Outs NSA Spy Room"*. Wired Magazine: July 2006. *http://archive.wired.com/science/discoveries/news/2006/04/70619* (accessed February 2014).

"Smart Highway". *http://www.studioroosegaarde.net/project/smart-highway/stories/#804* (accessed May 2014).

"Smartphone Users Worldwide Will Total 1.75 Billion in 2014". eMarketer: January 16, 2014. *http://www.emarketer.com/Article/Smartphone-Users-Worldwide-Will-Total-175-Billion-2014/1010536* (accessed September 2014).

Smith, Craig. *"By the Numbers: 64 Amazing Facebook User Statistics"*. Digital Marketing Ramblings: December, 2013. *http://expandedramblings.com/index.php/by-the-numbers-17-amazing-facebook-stats/#.UtMD3_v5OXM* (accessed January 20, 2014).

"Social Compliance: Protect Brand Equity and Ensure Governance". Aberdeen Group: January 2012.

Solis, Brian et al. *"The 2014 State of Digital Transformation"*. Altimeter Group: 2014.

"Statistics Brain". FaceBook. *http://www.statisticbrain.com/facebook-statistics/* (accessed January 20, 2014).

"Stolen Facebook and Yahoo Passwords Dumped Online". <u>BBC News</u>: December 4, 2013. *http://www.bbc.co.uk/news/ technology-25213846* (accessed January 2014).

"The C-suite Challenges IT: New Expectations for Business Value". Economist Intelligent Unit. <u>The Economist</u>: June 13, 2012. *http://www.slideshare.net/Management-Thinking/the-csuite-challenges-it-new-expectations-for-business-value* (accessed August 2014).

"The Digital Advantage: How Digital Leaders Outperform their Peers in Every Industry". Gapgemini Consulting and the MIT Center for Digital Business: 2012.

"The Digital Consumer". The Nielsen Company: February 2014.

"The Internet of Things: The Future of Consumer Adoption". Acquity Group: 2014.

"The President's SAVE Award". The White House. *http://www.whitehouse.gov/save-award* (accessed February 2014).

"The Rise of Content Marketing: Invest in Content Management and Development for Success". Forrester Research: September 2012.

"The True Cost of Compliance". Ponemon Institute: January 2011. *http://www.tripwire.com/tripwire/assets/File/ponemon/True_Cost_of_Compliance_Report.pdf* (accessed July 2014).

"The World in 2013: ICT Facts and Figures". International Telecommunication Union (ITU). *http://www.itu.int/en/ITU-D/Statistics/Pages/facts/default.aspx* (accessed December 2013).

"Threat Horizon 2016". Information Security Forum (ISF): 2014.

Titze, Christian, and Ray Barger Jr. *"How to Enable End-to-End Supply Chain Visibility"*. Gartner, Inc.: January 23, 2014.

Titze, Christian, William McNeill, and Ray Barger Jr. *"Multiple Processes, Partners and Data Objects Must be Considered to Obtain Benefits from Supply Chain Visibility"*. Gartner, Inc.: July 25, 2013.

"Top 10 Largest Economies in 2020". Euromonitor International from IMP: July 7, 2010, *http://blog.euromonitor.com/2010/07/special-report-top-10-largest-economies-in-2020.html* (accessed July 2014).

"Trace My Shadow". Tactical Technology Collective. *https://myshadow.org/trace-my-shadow* (accessed September 2014).

"Transform Your Business With the Nexus of Forces". Gartner, Inc.: February, 2014.

"Transitioning to Workforce 2020". Cisco: 2011. *http://www.cisco.com/web/learning/employer_resources/pdfs/Workforce_2020_White_Paper.pdf* (accessed July 2014).

Tulgan, Bruce. *"Meet Generation Z: The Second Generation Within the Giant "Millennial" Cohort".* RainmakerThinking, Inc.: November 6, 2013. *http://rainmakerthinking.com/assets/uploads/2013/10/Gen-Z-Whitepaper.pdf* (accessed August, 2014).

Turnbull, Malcolm. *"Australian Minister Calls for Innovation in Digital Media".* FutureGov Summit Australia: December, 2013. *http://www.futuregov.asia/articles/2013/dec/04/australian-minister-calls-innovation-digital-gover/* (accessed February 2014).

"Unleashing the Power of Information". CIO Magazine: 2012.

"U.S. Postal Service in trouble, losing $25 million daily". CNN: Dec 10, 2012. *http://outfront.blogs.cnn.com/2012/12/10/u-s-postal-service-in-trouble-losing-25-million-daily/* (accessed Jan 2014).

VanBoskirk, Shar. *"How to Organize for the Digital Future".* Forrester Research: March 7, 2013.

Vincent, James. *"Scientists Achieve Quantum Teleportation Breakthrough that could Prove Einstein Wrong".* The Independent: May 30, 2014. *http://www.independent.co.uk/news/science/scientists-achieve-quantum-teleportation-breakthrough-that-could-prove-einstein-wrong-9462053.html* (accessed July 2014).

Violino, Bob. *"Information Security Spending to Reach $71 Billion in 2014".* Information Management: August 25, 2014. *http://www.information-management.com/news/information-security-spending-to-reach-71-billion-in-2014-10026010-1.html* (accessed August 2014).

Viswanadham, N. *"Orchestration: The New Form of Collaboration".* InsightOn. *http://drona.csa.iisc.ernet.in/~nv/41%20Orchestration%20InsightOn_E-Commerce%20and%20Collaboration.pdf* (accessed July, 2014).

Wardley, Simon. *"Cloud Computing - Why IT Matters".* YouTube: 2009.

Weintraub, Alan. *"Create Your Information Governance Framework".* Forrester Research: August 7, 2012.

"What Exactly Is The "Internet of Things?" Infographic, Harbour Research and Postscapes. *http://postscapes.com/what-exactly-is-the-internet-of-things-infographic* (accessed March 2014).

"What We've Heard: Blueprint 2020 Summary Interim Progress Report". Government of Canada. November 2013.

White, Andrew. *"Information Governance and MDM Programs Key Initiative Overview".* Gartner, Inc.: April 23, 2014.

Woodward, Alys and Carla Arend. *"OpenText in Europe: Information Governance and Cultural Transformation"*. IDC: April 22, 2014.

"Working Paper: Digital Economy - Facts & Figures". Expert Group on the Taxation of the Digital Economy, European Commission: March 2014. *http://ec.europa.eu/taxation_customs/resources/documents/taxation/gen_info/good_governance_matters/digital/2014-03-13_fact_figures.pdf* (accessed May 2014).

"Young Girl Receives Lifesaving Windpipe Transplant Made From Her Stem Cells". Oristem: May 1, 2013. *http://www.oristem.com/uk/en/index.php/component/story/?view=storyview&Itemid=133&article_id=340#.U3yqXfldVJM* (Accessed May 2014).

"YouTube Statistics". <u>YouTube</u>. *http://www.youtube.com/yt/press/statistics.html* (accessed January 20, 2014).

"2012 Cisco Connected World Technology Report". Cisco: 2012. *http://www.cisco.com/c/en/us/solutions/enterprise/connected-world-technology-report/index.html* (accessed June, 2014).

"5G: A Technology Vision". Huawei Technologies Co., Ltd.: 2013. *"CEO Briefing 2014"*, Accenture, Global Agenda: 2014.

"7 Ways the Mobile Consumer Changes Everything". Bazaarvoice: 2014.

INDEX

Index